How Tall Are You?

Greg Morton

Text & Jacket Art Copyright © 2018 by Greg Morton

All Photographs Copyright © 2018 Greg Morton

All Rights Reserved.

Published by Morton Design Works

Printed in the U.S.A.

First Printing, 2018

This book began on Tuesday, October 25, 2016. Memorable, in part, because my beloved Chicago Cubs were appearing in the World Series against the American League Cleveland Indians. Feels so good to write that.

I have a good friend, his name is David. I met David in 2013 at the Garland Hotel to celebrate the 30th anniversary of the CBS hit television show Scarecrow and Mrs. King. I was lucky enough to be there as a cast member of the show. David, as a fan of the show. If you get to meet him, you'll find David is a great guy with detailed memories, fun stories and energy to spare.

His passion is Scarecrow and Mrs. King.

Over the course of a couple of years we continued to talk. In that time, my wife and I have grown close with David, though he lives in New Mexico and we in Southern California. One evening, while my Cubbies were preparing for the biggest start to a series in their young lives, I was on the phone with my friend David. That's where this book began. As an idea. From a fan.

Maybe I'm getting ahead of myself. You may have just picked this book up and wondered...Who is this guy? Yeah, I get that a lot. So, let's begin at the beginning.

I was on television. As a child.

Really, if I tell you more than that it's basically the CliffsNotes version and then you'd miss out on all of the really great (and funny) stuff in the rest of the book.

This is a memoir, of sorts. To the best of my ability, I'll share with you stories from my time on television. I'll also share some of the memorabilia that I've collected along the way, and what the entire experience has meant to me. My most treasured memorabilia? The fan mail I received as a child actor, all of which I've kept. In the grand scheme of my 15 minutes of fame, my mom always taught me to have respect for the fans. Without you, celebrities, even part time non-celebrities like me, wouldn't have a job.

This is my letter to you, to say thank you for being a fan.

I hope you enjoy.

For Jeanette Valliere,
Your passion and dedication does not go unnoticed.
Thank you, for keeping the fires burning.

For David Johnson,
Thank you, for being a friend, and a fan, and for helping me understand the importance of making a difference. This book is your fault. I mean that with love and admiration. Unless people hate it.
Then I mean it the other way.

The TRUTH IS...

...I've forgotten more than I can remember.

Not a great way to start a memoir, I know. But we have to have a relationship based on honesty, because when you do read the stories in this book I want you to know they're real. And they are real, to the best of my memory, and to the best of the memory of those I love and trust to remember such things.

Well, they're mostly real.

There are a few things to keep in mind about this period. It was brief. I haven't always cherished this part of my life, but I have always been appreciative of it. Also, it was a long time ago. I'm not old, by any stretch, but I was a child actor. Started way, way back in 1982 when I was nine. My career pretty much ended in 1987. I was 14. It was a whirlwind time that included work, celebrity and puberty.

How Tall Are You?

You can expect to find that, for this book, I'll often write like I talk. Which is to say that I digress. I'm all over the place at times. There isn't one track. You get the point.

I've learned over the years I'm a late bloomer. By that I mean, I am prone to mistakes, say a lot of stupid things, generally make a fool of myself, and then come out the other end wiser and better for the experience. I think you'll find in the following pages this is an apt description.

Mostly the making a fool of myself.

The DREAMER

I can be a pretty intense guy. As I've gotten older, I've realized that maybe I'm high strung, but not really sure what all that means. If you're getting the impression that writing is therapy for me, you'd be right. Just don't put me into one category or label me one thing. Unless you're going to label me a dreamer.

I admit that I can be pretty intense because I take certain things in my life seriously. Work and family more than anything else. I've made mistakes in both areas, but not for lack of trying. And really, that's kind of the point I'm trying to get across is that I take care of my responsibilities. That's important for me because, at my core, I am a dreamer.

My imagination takes me to far off places or invents little worlds for me to explore on a daily basis. Even if for mere moments. I love the fantasy of imagination. I had recently watched the Matt Damon movie "Jason Bourne" on a flight back to LAX. When the plane landed and my wife Sandra and I were walking through the terminal, I imagined I was an operative on a black ops mission trying to navigate the airport without being discovered. *Who were my enemies? Which pair of eyes were trained on me?*

For the most part, I think my day-dreams are harmless exercises for my brain. Other times I think they are a necessary exercise for my growth and development, not only as an artist but as a person. My day-dreams help give me a perspective on the world around me that I might not otherwise see through the lens of "reality". When I type this out, it seems absurd, and yet I'm not one bit ashamed to remain true to myself.

My dreams extend beyond mere fantasy of walking through an airport pretending I'm Jason Bourne. Being a day-dreamer means being able to explore or live out someone else's goals. As a young boy I always fantasized about adventures high up in the mountains, in far off lands. I haven't yet accomplished the far off lands, but I do venture up in to the mountains when I can. Day-dreaming helped me to achieve that goal. Day-dreaming keeps pushing me to one day see those mountains in a far off land.

How Tall Are You?

Having an active imagination is healthy, and has given me an outlet for the energy I've always had. I didn't know it when I was six, but my dreams were just the start of a journey for me into a world of imagination and creativity that I've explored ever since. Being a day-dreamer saved me from just being a hyper kid with no direction. I'm lucky my parents didn't discourage my play as a child, even when I would spend countless hours in the back yard by myself, surrounded by Star Wars action figures and dreaming about far off lands.

FAN MAIL

As I had mentioned earlier, this book is for the fans of mine and of Scarecrow and Mrs. King. If it wasn't for the fans, I probably would have never set out to write a *memoir*. But even if these stories reach just a few people, the effort was worth it. I have fan letters from my time on the show, how many people can say they've gotten fan mail?

Throughout this book I'm going to highlight each and every letter. Not the letters in their entirety, but a little something. As you'll note from the title of this book, my height was sometimes a thing. For some reason my height had gotten printed in a bio of mine and for many fans, it just stuck. Truth is, I'm short. But so is my wife, and so I think life has managed to work itself out. But...I am taller than my children, and that's all anyone can ask for, isn't it? Often, that little something in the letter turns out to be that girls thought I was cute. So let's talk about that for a moment.

How Tall Are You?

I'm a pretty self-aware guy. I'm confident, which many have perceived over the course of my lifetime as arrogant. I am, at times, full of myself. But I'm also self-aware enough to know the joke is on me from time to time. Often, I'm the one telling the joke. Though I may be confident in myself and my abilities, I don't pretend to be better than anyone else.

My confidence in large part comes from being bullied in school. I was on television when I hit those super awkward teen years. I was short, skinny, had a large head with unruly hair, braces on my teeth and spectacles. Adult size spectacles that when you look at the pictures now, you'll see those spectacles are wearing ME. Even without being on television, kids can be cruel at that age. The fact is, I often didn't know how to respond to the name calling or the feeling like I was an outsider. My DNA only knows one coping mechanism...Confidence.

Why am I telling you this? Two reasons, in order of least important to most important. First, you'll discover that, at times, I was a little shit. I may tell you stories about how that confidence got me into trouble. How I had basically opened my oversized mouth and fit my hobbit foot neatly into it. I'm human, prone to hubris. As an adult, I think some of these stories are funny, but that doesn't make me proud of my behavior. But they're my stories, and thus, they are me.

More importantly, I'm telling you about my coping mechanism because I worry there are people out there who don't have the same ability to rise above what other people are saying to them. Bullying, in all its degrees at work, at school or at home, grinds on people. I want to tell you that I understand. Words have incredible impact on what we perceive to be our identity.

Each one of us has the strength to persevere. At those moments when we least believe we have worth, we must find shelter in the aspects of ourselves we love the most. Our love of art, of movies, of literature, of science, the outdoors, animals, numbers, music. We all have a passion, whatever it may be. Something that makes us happy. Even in our darkest moments, our solitary moments, happiness is still reaching out. If you know what I'm talking about, please make the effort to persevere. You're worth it.

I found strength in knowing that others recognized my efforts. I've never thought I was cute or a great actor. The kids at school never said those things to me. But every once in a while I'd get a letter. From a fan.

There is a great big world out there, and we all have a place in it.

Finally, I want to add that, in this book, I'll type out these letters the best I can, in terms of spelling, punctuation and emphasis. I was a child, and as such I got a lot of letters from children. The spelling isn't great at times, and that is to be expected. I want to be clear of something when you read these imperfections...To me, they are perfect. Each misspelling or awkwardly phrased sentence is endearing, and the reason I love these letters so much.

I laugh at these letters, thirty years after I've received them. They are funny. I hope we can all laugh at them, and appreciate where we were so long ago. They are a part of my "yearbook" from my childhood. Who hasn't looked at their yearbook and laughed at the hair or the quotes or the clothes. Or the hair.

Truth is, I wouldn't want them any other way.

The DREAM

I had this dream. This one dream where something weird happened. It's pretty much stayed with me the rest of my life. That *something*. No, don't worry, I'm not going to light some incense, massage a crystal, listen to Enya and recall my previous lives. Grind my own coffee. Hug a tree.

Maybe we've all had that one dream. I have.

I was born in Milwaukee, Wisconsin. The time it will take you to read this paragraph will most likely be longer than the time I spent in Milwaukee. And I've never been back. From the stories my mom and dad have told me, it was kind of a strange time. My parents, with my older brother Jeff in tow, had relocated to Milwaukee for my dad's job. My maternal grandfather had passed away not a year before, so my mom was still grieving that loss. It was a cold Friday in January. I was born in a Jewish hospital. My parents aren't Jewish. Not that any of this really matters, but if you were going to write a sitcom about a high strung short kid from the Midwest, isn't this how you'd start?

We were in Milwaukee for five weeks after I was born. Five weeks. Long enough for me to experience winter on the lake, drink a Pabst, eat some cheese and get out of town. Of course, next stop was Chicago. Chicago! For about two years. Then on to the tropical paradise that is Ohio. I kid because, honestly, I've lived in Southern California for nearly 38 years and it's difficult for me to imagine I was born and nearly raised a snow ambivalent Midwesterner. Not that it matters, because I have no recollection of my life prior to Cincinnati. And then, mostly just the dream.

Allow me to digress, for a moment. As if I haven't already.

You'll find that I'm a dreamer. But what I'm not is a dreamer. Meaning, I don't generally have dreams or more specifically, I rarely remember them. It hasn't always been that way, but for the better part of my life I have not been one to remember my dreams.

Growing up in California, Claremont to be exact, I can sit here and picture my bedroom as if I was still there. My bed was pushed up against the corner of the room, and ran length-wise underneath a sliding glass window. My desk was at the foot of my bed. The closet across the room, next to the door. This is where I've had most of my dreams. When I remembered them.

My parent's room was an immediate right outside of my bedroom door, our two rooms sharing a common wall. Many nights I could hear the television as they watched before going to sleep. When I thought I could get away with it, I'd crawl on my belly like I was in basic training and camp myself at the foot of their bed as they watched The Tonight Show with Johnny Carson. Johnny remains my favorite television personality.

In the summer, my mom would wake in the morning to find me lying twelve inches from the box fan we ran in the hallway when it was hot outside. The white noise and cold air put me to sleep almost instantly. Like lying in front of a jet engine on the tarmac in Dubuque on a clear night in February. I think the fan was a coping mechanism. At that time, I had one reoccurring dream that I'll never forget. That dream where you wake up from bed, go to the bedroom window, draw up the blinds and someone is standing there looking right at you. Then you wake up, in a panic, and the last thing you want to do is actually get out of bed, draw the blinds and check.

Yeah, get all Freudian on that one. Spooky, right?

Needless to say, I was pretty thankful as a child to not remember my dreams all that often. I was never really whisked away to some wildly fantastic dreamland where I'd see and do wonderful things. A scary dream here and there, and that was it. But this was in Claremont, at least a year or so after I'd had the one dream I'd truly never forget.

It was my birthday. January, 1979. Cincinnati, Ohio. When I woke up that morning, I was six years old. Six! Oh, the possibilities ahead of me. The new adventures that would await. Like gifts! Cake! A party?!? I couldn't wait, and yet, something bothered me. I had this feeling like I'd already experienced something different. My dream hadn't been just a dream. It had seemed real. Frightening, almost, but not in the way a bogeyman might frighten. It was just...real. I had spoken with, interacted with, I mean it was a real experience...

I had just met Kate Jackson.

I know, right? Kate Jackson? A six year old has a life-altering dream and it's about Kate Jackson? I could have been dreaming about Star Wars, tying my shoe, riding a Big Wheel, or playing in the snow. It was, after all, January. All the things a newly minted six-year-old could be dreaming about, mine involved Kate Jackson.

Now you kind of understand why it kind of freaked me out. I mean, listen...Kate was really everyone's favorite Angel. (Charlie's Angels, kids. Look it up.) Seriously. Don't get me wrong, Farrah and Jaclyn were both great actors and beautiful, but come on. We're talking about Sabrina Duncan. The smart one. Everyone loves the smart one. As a family we watched the show, but I still don't understand why, at six, I was dreaming about Kate Jackson.

If you had asked me about dreams a year later, I probably wouldn't have remembered. At the very least, I wouldn't have admitted it. Maybe I was too young to understand or maybe once I had gotten to Claremont and started having that reoccurring nightmare I had just forgotten about Kate Jackson.

Today, I can't recall the specifics of the dream other than to say that in it, she was close. Close enough to touch.

Like a mother to a child. There was a warmth that, if anything, remains. Why the hell would a six year old dream of Kate Jackson? To this day, I still do not know.

Anyone who knows me well, knows I have a thing for smart brunettes. I married one. Maybe this fascination with beautiful, smart, dark haired crime fighters started at an early age. I'm just not buying it. Maybe this *is* the part of the book where I burn an incense stick and convince you my dream had some mystical, powerful origin.

Like fate.

ALABAMA

"Dear Greg,

Hi Hey Hello Whats up.

...It's 8:30 so my handwriting won't be the best.

...Greg, I love your TV show it's Great!!!!!

Sorry So Short

Sorry So Sloppy

Don't Do Drugs I don't"

Christie B.

Clanton, AL

Christie, my lone fan from Alabama. She included a picture of herself, and asked how old I was and what grade. Her letter was also stamped, repeatedly, with a red stamp that reads "Go For It". I imagine that now Christie works writing editions of thesauruses.

The postmark was January 23rd, 1985. At that time I would have been twelve years old, and probably in the sixth grade. For the record, I accept Christie's apology for the letter being so short, and so sloppy. Who knows if I otherwise would have forgiven such a faux pas, but she did basically begin with the disclaimer that it was 8:30. In truth, it was the five exclamation points that she loves my TV show that put her in good graces.

And Christie, I did go for it. Broke my arm once going for it. Fell down a mountain once going for it. Married my wife once going for it. You lose some, you win some. I appreciate the advice!

ARIZONA

"Dear Greg,

...I was writing to ask you how you got from commercials to the series Scarecrow and Mrs. King?

...What was it like moving from Wis. to Calif?"

Catherine D.

Tucson, AZ

"Dear Greg,

This is one of you fan.

...If you in Phoenix. Some day I would like to knew."

Mark J.

Queens Creek, AZ

"Dear Greg Morton,

How long does it take to memorize your part on Scarecrow and Mrs. King is if fun or scary do you Like it or not how old are you...

...I think the way you smile is cute and so are you i sorta have a crush on you....

...I think your cute. By: your #1 fan

P.S. I love you"

Misti P.

Douglas, AZ

In general, people who wrote to me, all kids themselves I'm sure, wrote on various kinds of notebook paper. Catherine sent a card, with an illustration of a kitty snuggling with a puppy on the front. She had asked about my move from Milwaukee to California, and at the ripe old age of eleven had, herself, never moved. Catherine, I moved from Milwaukee, Wisconsin to Hinsdale, Illinois, then to LaGrange Highlands, Illinois, then to Bedford Township, Michigan (just outside of Toledo, Ohio) and then Cincinnati, Ohio, Westchester, to be exact, before moving to Claremont, California. Aren't you glad you asked? What was it like? It was a lot of packing.

At this point in writing, I don't think I've re-read every letter, but I'm confident that Mark holds the record for the shortest. Three sentences in all. He never mentioned his age, but I surmise three sentences was the maximum output for his attention span at the time. Alabama Christie's letter was War and Peace compared to Mark's letter.

How Tall Are You?

Misti was in love, and another to make note of my height in her letter. I'm not sure if being 4' 4" was in my favor or not, but Misti felt compelled to mention it. She also felt compelled to add an "I (heart) You" sticker to the letter, and write "I love you" on the outside of the envelope. Where was this girl when I was fifteen and girls wouldn't give me the time of day? Douglas, Arizona, I guess.

One thing Misti wasn't big on was punctuation. I think her entire letter is one sentence. No worries. To answer her questions, I thought being on the show was fun and scary. It can be intimidating having to remember your lines in front of all those people who are sitting or standing behind the camera, staring at you. I not only liked it, I loved it. Every bit of it. The fun and the fear.

As far as how long it took me to remember my lines? That's a funny story. But I don't want to get ahead of myself. Read on!

A MONKEY in the STREET

I've never considered myself an actor.

In part because I never thought I was that good an actor. People tell me otherwise, but I guess it's just one of those things I have a tough time seeing. People tend to be their own greatest critics. For me, however, it goes beyond that.

I dug through a lot of old pictures in researching this book. One thing I discovered or rather, rediscovered, is that I'm a ham. A clown. You can see it in most, if not all, of the pictures of me over the years. Even before my years on television, I played to the camera when it was pointed at me. It was never the camera itself that was the center of my focus, it was the person behind it.

Since I was very little, I've had the ability to make people laugh. I think being cute had something to do with it, but there has always been a personality behind it as well. Once I learned I could make people laugh and smile, it became like a drug. I wanted to be the center of attention so that I could do what felt so natural.

It is a double edged sword, especially when you're six, seven and eight. Those years were the real turning point for me and my perception of who I am. The Catch-22 is that you want to make people laugh, but you have to be the center of attention to do it, and that you have to be the center of attention first, in order to make people laugh. You can't just walk into a room and make people laugh. They have to notice you first. And once they notice you, you'd better start being funny. There are few things worse than grabbing the spotlight and then dying on stage.

It's the age old fear of any comic, right? It's one reason I've never even considered Stand-Up as a career. I've walked into a room and commanded everyone's attention before, only to hear crickets. And that was a room of people I knew. A small room, with no spotlight or real expectation. Just me, making a fool out of myself, and then slinking on out of the room.

That was a regular occurrence for me in Junior High. I was in the middle of the high of being a professional performer, and thought I could just muscle my way into the hearts and minds of my fellow hormone rattled teenagers. I'll be the first to tell you it doesn't work that way, especially when you don't do the performance part well.

It takes skill to command a room. A skill that begins with natural talent, but you have to hone it. Practice it. Professionals, to this day, go out and work out new material on a live audience. You have to work out the kinks. Thirteen and fourteen year old me didn't know this. Open Mouth: Insert Foot. It didn't help that I was crazy for girls, and thought I could swoon them with my funny. You can't just walk in and make it happen. Unless you're six.

The cute thing comes in real handy when you barge into a room full of your parents' friends, hair disheveled just right, footy jammies scraping across the tile floor, just the right joke that is borderline inappropriate for a little kid to be telling, but telling it just perfect to get everyone rolling on the floor in laughter. Right before mom steps in, clearing the tears from her eyes, and shooing you back to bed.

Of course, not every night like that was a success. Sometimes I'd just end up being the little kid that was acting crazy by walking on the knuckles of his toes or doing weird flips because all of my other material wasn't working. At that age it was a little tough to censor myself and be more discerning about what worked and what didn't. At that age, I'd end up just pushing the envelope.

Risk Taker. It is one of the characteristics that most, if not all, performers share. You have to be willing to put yourself out there and look like a fool, because sometimes there is a fine line between foolish and entertainment gold. You'll never get there, however, without the risk. Though I don't prefer labels, being a risk taker is one of the reasons I consider myself more of an entertainer than an actor.

Maybe I never got the chance, as my acting career had a short shelf life, but I don't feel I ever took risks as an actor. Many of the good actors do. They put themselves out there for roles that are funny or dramatic and take big risks in their performances. I was a child, playing a child. In every role.

I haven't done scripted work since I was a teenager. As an adult, professionally I've done hosting work in front of the camera, and a lot of behind the scenes work. I've also done a lot of public speaking over the years, such as presentations, classrooms and autograph sessions. Put me in front of people, and the entertainer appears, ready to work. Who knows, maybe someday I'll find myself back in front of the camera doing scripted work, and find that I really am an actor.

ARKANSAS

"Dear Greg,
...I'm an avid fan of **Scarecrow and Mrs. King***!!*
It's been my favorite show most of the time it's been on
and I wouldn't miss it for the world!
...Your fan till Niagra Falls,"

Laura H.

Van Buren, AR

Laura typed her letter, and printed it in good ole fashioned dot matrix. It is post marked 1986. She was quite inquisitive, asking me how life is, what other work I'd done, how long I'd been acting, if I had a girlfriend, when my birthday was and where I was born, and what my hobbies were.

I love that she signed off "till Niagra Falls". People rarely speak that way, and when they do, we think they're weird. Personally, I love it.

I realize it's 30 years late, but Laura, this book is for you and every other fan out there who had the same questions.

CALIFORNIA

"Dear Greg,

...I have a few things to ask you. 1. How long have you been acting? Please write back."

Jacinda A.
Torrance, CA

"Dear Gregg Morton,

HI! Congradulations on having a fantastic show, Scarecrow and Mrs King!

...In fact, we love it soooo much, we made a private fan club for you!

...More about the club. We've already written to Kate Jackson, Bruce Boxleitner, Paul Stout, Beverly Garland and Martha Smith, but soon will write to Mel Steward. So far we haven't done any activities yet."

Supervisor: Cressie P.
President: Elanna P.
Vice-President: Eliana E.
Treasurer: Joey B.

Attendees: Corey D.
Activities Director: Kathy C.
Pomona, CA

"Dear Greg:
...I like you. You are very, very talented. I like
"Jamie" a lot. He is very nice and very, very funny."

Susan D.
Thousand Oaks, CA

"Hi Greg,
My two sons Aaron 5 and Arik 4 years old and I watch
you on Scarecrow every week. We all really love the
show."

Aaron, Arik and Linda R.
Madera, CA

Sweet Jacinda. She wanted to ask me so many questions, and only one made the cut. Her letter didn't come with an envelope (or I've since lost it), so unfortunately I don't have a postmark. Regardless, I started in 1982. That should give you a head start on the math.

Jamie *was* very, very funny. I was typecast. I'm good with it.

The letter from the private fan club was written by President Elanna P., by all accounts. It was mailed from Pomona, California (about 40 miles from Burbank where we filmed the show) to CBS Studios in New York, New York. All on a 22 cent stamp. I don't know why I'm fascinated by that, but I am. Also, Pomona is the next town over from Claremont, where I lived at the time. *They were so close.*

Anyway, at the time they'd written a lot of letters (that had probably traveled a lot of miles) but hadn't done any other activities. What, may I ask, was Kathy doing this whole time??

In reflection, of all the things I'm proud of, I'm most proud of being a part of a show that was a family show. I hear that often from fans that they watched with their parents, and that they now watch with their kids. The family of Aaron, Arik and Linda is a great example of that.

MICKEY ROONEY'S TALENT TOWN, U.S.A.

I naturally have a lot of energy. And I like being the center of attention.

Imagine my mom's challenge of finding things for me to do when I wasn't in school. Back then, grade schoolers didn't have advanced level college courses and twelve hours of homework every night. I was nine. I needed something to do. No easy task.

My brother loved sports. Growing up, he played baseball, football, soccer. I still remember going with my mom to my brother's baseball games at College Park in Claremont and spending the entire time climbing in the trees or in and around the decommissioned rail engine that anchored one end of the park. Think of me as a hairless monkey.

Spring of 1982 I tried my hand at baseball. At one point I played every position on the team except pitcher. I remember liking the game, and being quite good at it, but to hear my mom talk about it, baseball wasn't my thing. To be honest, I'm not surprised. Reflecting back, I see how an organized team sport wouldn't hold my interest long enough. Maybe it was too many rules or maybe it was the pace or relying on others. I'm not sure. Baseball is my religion now. Has been my entire adult life, not that I play. But I enjoy being a spectator.

Soccer, too, wasn't my thing. This one I understand completely. I don't follow the game as an adult. I looked good in the uniform, but didn't care for all of the running. I think the ball scared me, too. I used to jump over it when it was kicked my direction. Not a great skill-set for a soccer player. Later I discovered I was a damn fine dodge-ball player, but that talent did little good on the soccer pitch. As it turns out, I didn't want to play sports as a child.

In the summer of 1982, knowing she'd be saddled with me for three straight months while school was out, mom enrolled me at Mickey Rooney's Talent Town, USA in Azusa, CA. It would be my first experience with professional instruction in entertainment. Not that I wanted to be left with a bunch of strangers. As my mom tells it, the first week I was enrolled I threw a temper tantrum each time she tried to drop me off.

As much as I'm an extrovert, I'm really not. I prefer to be alone. I'm a day-dreamer. I live in my own little fantasy world, making things up and being perfectly happy doing it. Uh, HULLO...I'm a fiction writer, for Pete's sake! I'm forty four years old and still daydreaming. I get nervous doing new things now, with new people and new experiences. The difference is that now I'm forty four years old. I've learned to accept new experiences. Relish them. Seek them out. I believe new experiences are the key to eternal youth. But, have this conversation with nine year old me and all you'll get is a temper tantrum.

I was nine, and my evil mother was getting rid of me because she either wanted me to play with other kids or was simply trying to get rid of me. I just knew it. How could she? OF COURSE I was throwing a temper tantrum!

No actor is a success solely on their own merits. It is a team effort to make things happen in Hollywood, no matter what anyone tells you. Actors have to be given advice, training or opportunities. Sure, the good ones are good. The pretty ones are pretty. *I'm talking to you, Brad Pitt.* But none of them get where they are alone. They have people to thank along the way. For me, I have to thank nobody more than my parents. But I also have to thank Carly Moultrie.

Carly Moultrie was from Claremont, my hometown. She had two daughters the same ages as my brother and me, and both of her kids were actors. Carly was an instructor at Mickey Rooney's Talent Town. Being a mother and an entertainer and a sane person with good hearing, she stepped in when my mom attempted to drag her son, kicking and screaming, through the doors to hopefully lose him forever.

Carly took me by the hand, gave me a reassuring smile to calm my nerves, winked at my mom and whisked me indoors where I found pure bliss amongst my people...The entertainers. *Cue the music. Montage of people smiling and laughing. End credits. OSCAR!*

It may not have been quite that dramatic, but that is essentially what happened. Carly took me by the hand and for the next few hours anyway, my mom found a peace she would not again enjoy until I moved out of the house.

When I say the Talent Town people were my people, I mean it. Everyone was goofy, nerdy, dorky, full of energy and willing to do just about anything to entertain you. My people. What most of them had that I didn't? Discipline. But that was why I was there.

Mind you, at this time in my life I could sing. Sort of. I mean, as much as a nine-year-old can sing. I was no Billy Gilman, but then again, I was no William Hung. That I could somewhat carry a tune was a good thing, considering the Talent Town was basically a song and dance troupe. So I became a song and dance man.

Author Note: My daughter informed me that my Gilman/Hung references were dated. Sigh. So am I. I don't feel old by any stretch, but let's face it, I was a child actor in the '80s. I love when she tries to make me cool.

My first gig with the group was as a poor orphan in the musical "Oliver!". Food, glorious food. Put me in makeup, second hand clothes, throw me on stage and watch me twirl around. Not bad, huh? I loved it. The rush of being on stage. The lights. The crowd. It was (and still is) an addiction.

There is nothing like being on stage. Nothing. Whether it is a classroom, a presentation, a Q&A, a musical or a play, performing in front of a live audience is the most thrilling experience in entertainment. The feedback from the audience is immediate. You know whether you suck or you don't.

Case in point. When I was in Junior High at El Roble, I took a drama class. Regrettably the only drama class I ever took. Our teacher, Mr. Kirkland, wrote a play that we performed before the end of the semester. I don't recall all of the details, but by this time I had been a professional actor on television. I was volunteered for the part of the villain.

Basically, my character was a rip-off of the Snidely Whiplash character from the Dudley Do-Right cartoons during the Rocky and Bullwinkle Show on Saturday mornings. You know the guy...Top hat, curly mustache, always loses. That was my character in this play. My mom still has my top hat.

At one point in the show, I made my entrance to do my part to swoon the damsel before she spurns my advances and calamity ensues. I had seen people on television spray minty freshener in their mouth before kissing another person, so I had gotten my mom to buy me a small bottle of Binaca spray before our performance, and I had it tucked away in my costume.

How Tall Are You?

As I walked out on stage, my eyes squinted in the bright lights. I could barely see the audience. My heart raced. My palms grew sweaty. I feared I would forget any and all lines I was to recite. The only thing I could think about was that stupid little Binaca bottle in my pocket. I pulled it out, removed the cap, and sprayed two shots into my mouth. The crowd roared.

I was on cloud nine. My lines came rushing back to me and I breezed through the scene. I had killed it. Mr. Kirkland was ecstatic. I had improvised and it worked. He loved that sort of thing, encouraged it really. Maybe he even expected it from a "professional". I don't know for sure. I only know two things. 1) It seemed the only natural thing to do and 2) The crowd's reaction is as clear to me today as it was all those years ago.

Nothing beats the stage.

I learned that early on at Mickey Rooney's Talent Town. There is a hum to live theater. The energy of opening night is palpable. I vividly remember staging for the first act of "Oliver!" The house lights were on, and people were filing in. Backstage was a symphony of people, all bustling to get their jobs finished before curtain. The actors were nervous with excitement.

"Break a leg!"

"Don't forget your hat."

"Remember the words?" "Sure do!"

"I might have to pee."

As I stood there on the stage, the lights behind the curtain dimmed, I could feel this pulse. The quieting chatter of the audience. It was anticipation, for the entertainers and those who had come to be entertained. That pulse reveals itself in your ears, and in your palms and in your chest, and most definitely in your head. It is not just your heart racing. It is the stage.

When the house lights dim and everything is dark, the excitement is at its peak. And then the curtain slowly creeps open, the spotlights hit the stage in a brilliant flash! *You're on, you're on!! Music. Verse, and step. Don't bump into that kid like you did in rehearsal. Wow, the crowd is huge...Look at all those people. Just look at them. They're looking at me!*

"Oliver!" was just the beginning. I remember classes where we improvised scenes, just to get us thinking on our feet. We were paired off and given a basic scenario. One of us, as actors, would start the scene.   During improvisation, pretty much anything goes. If the other actor makes something up, you go with it. It is make-believe in pure form, and some of the most genuine fun I've ever had.

I've forgotten the horrible tragedies that my mother had imparted on me during that time of deceit and abandonment. I kid, of course. My mom is great. But, I have forgotten any memories of not wanting to attend the classes and only have fond memories. One of which was performing at the Los Angeles County Fair.

Ask me today if I recall the words to "I Don't Want to Grow Up" and the answer will be a definite no. Call it age or some Freudian thing where I don't want to remember. Ironically, I'd say that song is appropriate for how I've lived my life. I don't remember the words, but I do remember performing that song at the Los Angeles County Fair. Pretty cool, right? Me, a little 4H, some deep fried something or other. It all fits, no?

Mickey Rooney's Talent Town, USA. For me, it was where I learned to be a working actor. A professional entertainer. It was a beginning for me. Thanks to high energy, summers off, a mother in need of a break and Carly Moultrie.

FLORIDA

"Hi,
Hope you get this one.
...You are a great actor & so cute.
Take Care, Carma & Teresa"

Carma G.
Orlando, FL

"Dear Greg,
...I don't have much to say is
...Your are cute in the picher."

Gloria J.
Gonzalez, FL

"Tuesday
11/15/1983:
Dear Greg:
...Have for many years collected material on
entertainers and would like to ask you to send me an
autographed picture of yourself from the show."

"Saturday

9.22.1984:

Dear Greg:

...Have for many years collected..."

"Tuesday

10.9.1984:

Dear Greg:

...Have for many years collected..."

Joseph S.

Miami, FL

In December of 1983, Carma sent a plain white postcard to Hollywood from Orlando for $0.13. Based on her opening, I'm not sure her previous correspondence got to me. USPS reliability may have been a problem for Florida as a whole, if Joseph's four letters are any indication.

Gloria, bless her heart, must have been really young. Her spelling and grammar weren't the best, and she appeared quite conflicted in content. In the body of her letter she wrote, then scratched out, twice, that she thought I was cute, before finally admitting it on a small note on the side of the letter. She *didn't* have much to say, other than I was cute.

How Tall Are You?

But really, what else is there to say?

Joseph was...Persistent. Looking at the initial envelope from 1983, I'm not convinced we received it any time close to when he sent it. It was graffitied with several stamps and postmarks. That may account for the next two nearly identical letters, mailed seventeen days apart. Through wind or rain or sleet or dark of night, Joseph wanted his autograph. I know that because, well, he also mailed his business card that listed Joseph as, what else? Photographer and Autograph Collector.

GEORGIA

"Dear Jamie,

Could you send me ten autographed pictures of you?"

Dana C.
Douglas, GA

"Dear Greg morton,

...I thing you are cute.

...If you don't want to write back you don't have to. Please do."

Holly V.
Cartersville, GA

Dana was very inquisitive in her letter, asking me how old I was, when my birthday is, and what my middle name is. What struck me most was that she asked for ten autographed pictures. Ten. I don't want to be presumptuous, but I'm pretty sure she was going to sell them on the black market. That is, the black top. At school. She was probably telling the kids they were buying autographed pictures of Danny Pintauro.

Holly was ten at the time she wrote me. Her letter was a full page, neat, and in cursive. Spelling wasn't perfect, but at ten years old, all is forgiven. If you're in your forties now and can't tweet the difference between "you're" and "your", well, then, that's a different story. What freaked me out about reading Holly's letter all these years later? The post script. It reads "P.s. are you relly 44 and".

Obviously, an incomplete thought. However...I happen to be 44 years old (at the initial time of writing). This book is taking longer than I thought. I either had more to share than I thought or I'm one giant windbag. I'm going with windbag.

Anyway, my guess is that Holly was referring to my height, which somehow seemed to be a thing with the fans. Was I 4' 4"? At one time, yes. Why was that part of my bio? The pitfalls of not having a publicist, I guess. Still, weird to see that on a piece of paper today.

TONI KELMAN and ASSOCIATES

I'd been on stage in musicals, and musical numbers. I was a song and dance man. Well, song and dance boy. I'd been performing in my living room for family and friends for years. Being in front of people, making them laugh and entertaining them, was where I was most comfortable. And to some degree, still.

But I was a starving actor. I worked odd jobs like sanitation and in a kitchen to pay for room and board from a couple I rented a room from. I didn't have a car. I wasn't getting a lot of gigs. Life was tough.

It wasn't. I was a child living at home, doing chores.

I *was* doing well with Mickey Rooney's Talent Town, USA. I had gotten over my fear of going, to my mom's delight, and I was having fun. I was a performer! Meeting new friends, experiencing new things. I had found my place. Except...

There is a natural progression in being a performer. I call it a natural progression, but it in many ways is an ambition. A desire to discover new worlds. That progression happened to me. First the living room, and then opportunities to perform popped up at school, like the Spring Sing. It was an organized, choreographed stage recital, something I had never done before. The Spring Sing was a learning experience. A growth experience. I loved it.

There isn't the same sense of creativity and individuality on the baseball diamond as there is on the stage. It's no wonder I kept gravitating toward the stage. Any stage. With the progression in performing, the stage gets bigger, and so does the audience. There is a drive to entertain more people. I have to say, too, the experiences are pretty cool. I'm in awe of the process, as much as the end product. Don't get me wrong, my number one goal has always been to entertain. I'm an entertainer first. But part of the draw, the drive, the ambition, is in the process. That process was leading me from Claremont, to Azusa, to Hollywood.

Carly Moultrie saw something in me. A glimmer of something, anyway. On her recommendation, my mom called Hal Ralston, a professional photographer who specialized in talent photography. The headshot. Ever watch a corny movie or television show where the photographer is snapping away at the subject, talking to them the whole time?

"Lift your head."

"Smile."

"You're serious now. Serious."

"Ahh, that's great. Just great. You're going to be a STAR!"

Yeah...That's kind of how it happens. Except, not so dramatic.

My mom had arranged an outdoor photo session with Hal, a predetermined fee was agreed upon, and a date. Me? I was probably in my room at the time, lost in an epic battle of Star Wars figures or buried in Choose Your Own Adventure books. The date came, I hopped in the car, and away we went on a sunny Saturday afternoon to Griffith Park with a trunk full of clothes and "props".

"Lean against this tree."

"Hold this book. You're studying now. Studying."

"No, smile this time. Yeah, that's it."

"Ok, go change your clothes. Grab your skateboard when you come back."

That was pretty much it. Nobody in the park cared that a hobbit was getting his picture taken. Or standing on his head while some guy took his picture and his mom looked on in wonder. If you're in and around Hollywood, and you look close enough, you might just see the next Brad Pitt getting his pictures taken in the park. Not that I'm the next Brad Pitt, mind you. I'm pretty, but come on. Of course, everyone is busy taking their own pictures these days...so there's that.

Anyway, I'd done it. Gotten my headshots taken. Which, by the way, seems to me to be a morbid term. No? What is wrong with "picture" or "pictures"? Same number of syllables and one or two fewer letters. But I digress.

After a few days, we were shipped the proofs. I'd taken school pictures before, but look-out...These pictures made me look like a star! I was impressed. Amazed, even. I mean, this guy knew what he was doing!! He was, after all, a professional. All jokes aside, it showed. There is a difference between having your cousin Larry break out the Kodachrome at Thanksgiving and pop out back in the yard for a few glamour shots and having professional pictures taken by, that's right, a professional. You can see the difference, and so can a casting agent.

Or in my case initially, a talent agent.

Hal Ralston had forwarded the proofs of my photo session to Toni Kelman, head of her own talent agency, Toni Kelman & Associates. Toni specialized in representing child actors, and had represented Jodie Foster at one point. My star magnetism was clearly on display in my headshots...clearly, and Toni swept me up in a hurry before anyone else could get their hands on me. I was going places!

As far as I know, those last two sentences could be true. They probably aren't, but for the sake of argument we'll say that's how it went down, because honestly I don't remember. And neither does my mom. For dramatic purposes, and literary license, I'll fully commit to the "I was awesome" storyline. My book = My rules.

Let's be honest, though. I *was* cute. Adorable, even. It was my super power.

Looks account for 90% of talent at that age. So the agency took a chance on me, and I was assigned to Arletta

Proch, an associate. This was the fall of 1982. And it wouldn't be long before Arletta had moved the chess pieces and her newest asset was going to work.

ILLINOIS

"Dear Greg (Jamie),

I love you alot!!! I like the show too. I think you're cute!!!!

...Could you please tell me what you think of me? If you like me could you send a picture of yourself? I am always thinking about you."

Jody B.
Washington, IL

"Dear Greg,

...I think you play the part of Jamie great.

...Your acting is just as if you belong in the King family you play is so good.

...I would love to have an autograph photo of you to add to my collection of famous people."

Dorothy E.
Moline, IL

"Dear Greg,

...I like you and think you are a good actor.

How Tall Are You?

...I like to have a picture of you."

James E.
Andulusia, IL

"Dear Greg Morton,
I am saving pictures of my favorite movie stars, and
I was wondering if I could get one of you.
...I am very excited about starting this hobby."

Shirley E.
Rock Island, IL

"Dear Greg,
...My cousin goes coo-co over you. She is saying all
these things like Sandy Morton (ha-ha).
...Do you like being a T.V. star? Or would you like to
be a normal kid? How do you go to school when you are
acting so much?"

Wendy K.
Worth, IL

"Dear Greg,
...Your grandma went to the dentists office. She gave
my mom a picture of you. I thought it was real neat."

Sheri L.
Tremont, IL

"Dear Greg,

How Tall Are You?

...You're a great actor and have always been a favorite of mine. You're also quite handsome! Keep up the good work!!!"

Julee S.

Aurora, IL

"Dear Greg Morton,

I try to watch your show every Friday, and sometime it work out.

...What do you like and dislike?

...Have you ever flown with Paul in a helicopter yet?"

Cecil S.

Tovey, IL

"Dear Greg (Morton),

...I think you are a great actor.

...I am the same age as you and I think you are so <u>cute</u>!

...Again, I would like to tell you how cute you are!! That is why I would like to have a picture of you (autographed)."

Sandy S.

Oak Lawn, IL

How Tall Are You?

Author Note: Janet Watson wrote me a poem, using each letter of my first and last names as the beginning of each line of her poem. And it rhymed. Certainly the most creative fan letter I've ever gotten.

Janet W.

Granite City, IL

Jody, I think you are very sweet for taking the time to write me a letter. And I think it's great that you loved me but just liked the show.

I'm pretty sure Dorothy E. was the matriarch who started the autograph collection hobby in and around the Moline area. She, James and Shirley all share the same surname. Shirley typed her letter.

Wendy from Worth, Illinois...Coincidentally, I married a girl named Sandra. She goes coo-co over me too. Your cousin had the right idea, but I think geography was a problem in our relationship. By the way, I did like being a T.V. star, but honestly always thought it funny to be referred to that way. In my eyes, Paul Newman was a star. I was just me. And to your second question...I did want to be a normal kid. And I've regretted it for years.

How Tall Are You?

I'm surprised that I don't have more letters like Sheri's from Tremont. Tremont is a small town outside of Peoria, Illinois. Both of my grandmothers lived in Illinois during my lifetime. My maternal grandmother lived in Galesburg, and my paternal grandmother lived in Peoria. Both were very proud of me and my successes, and spent a lot of time talking about me to their friends (or anyone at the dentist, apparently). Grandparents are great that way, aren't they?

I have done my best to keep up the good work of being quite handsome, as Julee had requested. It hasn't been easy. It's hard work being quite handsome.

I'm thankful that for Cecil, it worked out sometimes that he was able to catch the show, because, you know, sometimes it doesn't. As far as what I like and dislike? Wow, that's an open ended question. Let's go with this, for now...I like baseball, the sound of the waves on the sand, the smell of freshly cut grass and my wife's laugh. Always my wife's laugh. Dislikes? The sound of auto accidents, the taste of lima beans and rude people.

How random to ask me if Paul and I had ever ridden in a helicopter. Uh, no. My first ride in a helicopter came when I had to be rescued off the top of a mountain. But that's a different book.

I wonder if Sandy S. is the girl who was coo-co over me. I may never know. She did mention quite a few times in her letter how cute I was, but it's hard for me to discern if she's just saying that for an autographed photo. Not that I'm complaining.

INDIANA

"Dear Greg,
...Your the Best on the show.
I like you smile and I Love you looks."

Jenny G.
Elhart, IN

Jenny's letter was eight lines and a post script. She did take the time to write, in giant letters across the massive amount of real estate at the bottom of the page "Write back." She was twelve at the time of writing, as noted by the fact that she told me. That, and how tall she was (taller than me), her hair color and her weight. Her weight.

Basically, Jenny's letter was a 1985 precursor to Tinder. If I had known I would never again have so many girls compliment me on how great I looked, I would have stayed twelve years old forever.

I have scanned the letter and sent it to the executives at CBS, just to remind them I was the "Best" on the show. Because Jenny said so.

RUSTLED into the PEN

The audition process for an actor like me is monotonous and repetitive, until it isn't. First, you get a call from your agent, who has gotten calls for kids my age, kids my gender, kids my color for a commercial or movie or pilot to be filmed for television. When one answers that call, it means driving to some obscure building somewhere in Hollywood or Burbank or (insert nearby town here) and walking in to a waiting room, headshot in hand, with twenty or so kids already there that look...Exactly...Like...You. Head for the desk, tell them you're there, get the scene you'll perform, go sit down.

Moo.

They call it a cattle call for a reason. Casting agents are fishing at this point (They should call it a fishing trip). They're looking for a "look" or a "thing". I bet if you ask them, even they don't know what they're looking for, other than they know the lead is a white female and the role calls for being the mother of two young boys, for example. So they cast the net for boys aged 10-13ish, brown or dark hair, you get the idea.

My super power managed to get me an audition. A lot of auditions. After school, in the car, down the freeway. Random building. A room full of me. Tell them your name, read the lines, thank you, have a nice day.

Moo.

Come back next week. Do it all over again.

Moo.

Then one day, you get a call from your agent. The producers called, they want to hire you! You've managed to herd yourself through the cattle call and into a job. It is the most exciting thing that can happen. You get calls from everyone you know congratulating you on being a star. Cops smile and wave at you as you drive 55 in a school zone. Unicorns bring you breakfast in bed.

What really happens is that your older brother punches you real hard in the arm and offers a "Congrats" as he immediately returns to not caring. The kids at school, too, don't care. No calls. No smiling cops. No unicorns. I basically remember nothing about getting hired for that first job.

I'm sure we were all ecstatic, my brother included. You have to remember, we were Midwesterners who had just come to California just a few years before. We had a taste of Hollywood that first day in August of 1979. We left Cincinnati in the pouring rain and arrived at sunny Los Angeles International Airport, where everyone was wearing shorts and t-shirts, the day was still warm, the exotic palm trees waved happily in the faint breeze and they were filming scenes from the upcoming movie "Airplane!" at the curb. True story.

After that first initial glimpse of Hollywood glamour at the airport, life in West Coast suburbia was pretty much the same as it had been in all of the other places we'd lived. School, work, neighbors, friends, life. My slow progression into the role of working actor was still inconceivable. You don't imagine where any of the auditions will actually take you, you just take life one day at a time. Yeah, I imagine that first phone call was pretty special.

I still don't remember it. I don't remember the job, either. I had gotten hired for a McDonald's in-house production. Essentially a commercial that would only be shown within the network of McDonald's corporate and franchisees. It was a one day shoot.

I don't know for sure, but I'm confident I played the role of a nine year old boy.

KANSAS

"Dear GREG,

Hi, I'm Krissi. Sorry I wrote, but when I saw your picture in our scrapbook I couldn't turn the page your picture was so cute.

...Alot of boys at school like me, but you don't have to.

P.S. A girl named April is going to write. She's a spoiled BRAT!"

Krissi F.

Douglass, KS

"Dear Greg,

...I saw you in the movie Scarecrow and Mrs. King. I think your cute.

...Are you going with anyone? Well if your not would like to go with me? I hope you like me the way I like you."

April P.

Douglass, KS

So...That happened.

Krissi and April mailed their letters the same day, May 13, 1985. I couldn't tell you which one I received first or which one I read before the other initially. I will say this, for the book I've gone alphabetically, assuming I'm not super tired when I'm writing, and so, Krissi F. came before April P. while compiling this book. To my surprise, it worked out the way it did. My wife and I have had a good laugh.

What has my curiosity piqued is this mysterious scrapbook that Krissi mentions. Where was my picture that they clipped it out of? Must have been a T.V. Guide, because in the four years I was on Scarecrow and Mrs. King, Teen Beat never came calling.

If they knew of the fierce love battle happening in Douglass, Kansas at the time, I may have been a cover-boy.

I was a working actor, but had worked a job that practically nobody would see. Looking back over my career, I know I had different expectations of what a career should look like. At that time, I thought being a working actor meant celebrity. That could be why I don't remember that first job, because nobody else remembers it.

In my eyes, my first true experience as a working actor came shortly before the holidays when I was hired for a national advertising campaign for the new Texas Instruments Speak & Spell. In May of 1982, one of the biggest movies of all time was released in theaters, directed by Steven Spielberg. E.T. The Extra-Terrestrial. In the movie, the titular character uses Elliot's digital toy to help phone home. If you haven't seen the movie, seriously, it's one of Spielberg's best.

The Speak & Spell had already been making waves in the technology industry for its innovative use of voice recall. When the movie was released, you couldn't find a person who hadn't seen it or not stopped talking about it. The movie helped catapult the toy into the stratosphere. See what I did there? Dad jokes galore in this book, so just buckle in. Anyway, Texas Instruments jumped on the chance to take advantage with a little creative advertising.

Movie tie-ins, as they call them, are nothing new. It is generally accepted that Spielberg's good friend George Lucas pioneered the modern day product licensing boom in Hollywood way back in 1977 when he released the original Star Wars. With licensing comes advertising tie-ins. Case in point, the E.T. Speak & Spell.

FADE FROM BLACK:

The camera rolls through the forest at night. We hear commercial announcer guy talking commercial stuff. We see a young child's toy. It's a Speak & Spell. A space ship! A close up of a young boy's face. A bright light!

FADE TO:

"Are you going to hog that all day?" says a young girl to her brother, who sits on the edge of a bed playing with the toy in question. We weren't in a forest, a young boy was dreaming! Announcer guy is still talking.

CUT TO:

END OF COMMERCIAL

Applause, applause, applause. One day shoot. I had a close-up and no lines. Perfect. Show my face, don't ask me to talk. What more could you ask from a job, really? I remember the lights. I always remember the lights. They're hot, I'm sure you know this. When you have a close up, and you're supposed to be looking at the bright light of a space ship, it can feel like you're in a tanning booth. Or the center of the sun.

The commercial was a huge success. They played the heck out of it on television. The job was easy. Basically, sit down, stare into the distance and pretend an alien ship is approaching (i.e. give'm big eyes), then sit on the edge of this bed and play with a toy while your "sister" says her line. Cut. Wrap.

I thought, *this acting thing was cake.*

And...I had finally gotten what I wanted out of being on television. Recognition.

I was a working actor!

Be careful what you wish for.

IOWA

"Dear Greg,

...I like the fact that "Jamie" and "Phillip" play an important part in each episode. I think you do a super job as "Jamie". You make him seem real."

Steven D.
Forest City, IA

"To Greg Morton,
From Talencia"

Talencia S.
Ames, IA

I was a method actor. I absolutely insisted the cast and crew treat me like a young boy even when I was off camera. I never broke character. Ever. My approach to acting inspired Daniel Day Lewis. That is how I made Jamie seem so real. Acting!

I kid, of course. For the most part I was trying to hit my marks, say my lines and not step in front of another actor during the scene. I didn't always succeed. More on that later. The one thing I did try my hardest? Stay calm. I think what many people perceive as reality was my attempt to stay calm.

As far as the kids playing an important role in the show. I actually have strong feelings about that. Is it selfish for me to say I think they should have had a bigger role in the show?

Talencia sent me a Christmas card, with an illustration of a sleeping baby, surrounded by a squirrel, a racoon, a rabbit, a lamb and one other cute, but wholly indistinguishable furry little creature. It was simple, but very sweet. Of course, now it bugs me that I can't identify the other animal.

I am JAMIE KING

Fun Fact: Another actor was originally cast in the role of Jamie King in the television series Scarecrow and Mrs. King.

Not Greg Morton.

I, myself, did not know this until just recently. In researching for this book, I discovered a few interesting things about me and the show. To say the least, this was the most shocking. I had always just assumed that I was one of many to heed the ring of a cattle call and shuffle through the process like any other job. But...Remember my dream? Fate, I guess.

I was a working actor. Bonafide. Friends and family had called the house to tell us they'd seen me on television. Kids at school had noticed, too. The Speak & Spell commercial was getting plenty of airplay. It felt good, so we kept auditioning through November. And December. Christmas Eve.

I was a child at this point, right? Nine years old, about to hit that all important milestone of double digits. Ten. I was working, sure, but really I was just a kid. My mind was almost singularly focused on play. Make believe. I was a dreamer. I was oblivious to the greater world around me. I wasn't concerning myself with work.

In Hollywood, as is the case with many things, you need to strike while the iron is hot. I was hot, so to speak. Having a current job airing on T.V. worked in my favor. My agent, Arletta, knew this. She kept running me out there for auditions. Including one on Christmas Eve. My dad had had enough.

A few things you should know about my dad. He was, hands down, my biggest supporter. My mom was essentially my manager, chauffeur, care-taker, shoo-er (that's one who shoos) and of course, mom. My dad was chief fan, financier of expenses, and keen watcher of my childhood. He loved that I was acting, but it wasn't about to interfere with our lives. His entire life he was focused on doing right by the family. It was bad enough that his own work kept him away as much as it did, he wasn't going to let this acting thing do the same. Especially on Christmas Eve.

How Tall Are You?

I don't remember the audition on the 24th. I didn't get the job, would that have made a difference? Maybe. Who knows? Regardless, we wouldn't have known if I had gotten the job or not on Christmas Eve, and anyway, it was Christmas Eve. Most of us let life get in the way of celebrating family and friends during the year, it was important we didn't do that during the holidays, as well. My dad called Arletta. We would not be going out on auditions for the next couple of weeks. It was our holiday break.

Thinking back, I don't have any memories of this period in my life. As I had mentioned before, I was most certainly preoccupied with kid-stuff. If I was upset that I couldn't go on auditions for a while, I don't remember. That's even if my parents told me. They probably didn't. They didn't need to consult with me.

So, Christmas came and went. New Year's too. I feel confident that being out of school for holiday break and not having to sit in a car for hours as we commuted to Hollywood or the surrounding cities was almost certainly a great thing for me. Stay up late, sleep in late, maybe swim in the pool. Books, games, toys. Chores. Ok, so maybe it wasn't Fantasy Island, but still, I'm sure it was great.

How Tall Are You?

New year, new opportunities. It was time to go back to work. Strike while the iron was room temperature, and all that. I had enjoyed some success, and was interested in pursuing more auditions. Arletta had one all lined up for me, but it's quite possible she had put her reputation on the line to do it.

During the holidays, producers of a new pilot to be filmed for CBS and Warner Bros. Television had cast the role of Jamie King, the youngest son of a divorced housewife who gets tangled up in the web of international espionage. It was a done deal. Except, Arletta told them they *had* to see me. They just had to.

They resisted.

Arletta didn't give up. That's what agents do, right? They fight for their clients. I had something. Arletta saw that in me, and she fought for me. She pushed CBS. You have to see this kid, she told them. Finally, they relented.

"We'll see him," they told her. "He better be good, because if not, we'll never use your agency again."

No pressure, right?

Luckily, we didn't know about any of this going in to audition. And so there I was. Me. No room full of doughboy haircuts and button noses. An appointment for one. On one side of the room, all this expectation about some kid an agent insisted they had to see and on the other a kid just playing make believe. Oblivious to just about everything.

I read lines for the casting agents. We spoke. It was an audition like any other. "Pretend this happens." "Say this." "How would you react if this character said that?" "Great." "Wait here." One person left. That person returned. "Let's go down the hall, I want you to meet someone." We all got up and left. Down the hall. "Greg, this is so and so..."

The audition lasted a couple of hours. As my mom tells the story, they kept shuttling me from room to room, introducing me to people. I read more lines. Answered more questions. In my young career, it was the longest audition I'd had. Finally, it was over. "Thanks for coming." "We appreciate your time." "Expect to hear something in the next several days."

They called us the next day. The producers at CBS wanted to meet. They wanted me to come back in and read with one of the cast members. I was going to meet Kate Jackson.

In my little world, few stars were bigger than Kate Jackson. So when I first got the chance to meet her, it was a realization that this acting thing could be something special. The experience left a lasting mark. I often speak of the opportunity to be a working actor in Hollywood, a rare feat in the grand scheme of things. Imagine meeting a world famous celebrity for the first time, not as a fan, but as a peer.

Don't get me wrong, a ten-year-old kid with little experience as an actor walking into a room with Sabrina Duncan isn't a peer in talent or resumé. But as actors, well, you have a job to do. And that was how I met Kate.

Fate, right? I'd dreamt that I would meet Kate Jackson, and here I was, about to audition for a part that had already been cast for a show with her. Would you believe I wasn't nervous? Maybe, just a little. But more than anything I remember feeling excited. And a little Deja-vu.

I walked into the audition and met another actor about my age, sitting with his mom. His name was Paul. He would be reading for the role of Phillip, the older brother. This kid looked like he could be my brother! It was the first moment in my life I knew I was in the right place at the right time. I hadn't forgotten the dream or if I had, it had suddenly come back to me in that moment. I wasn't intimidated. I was there for a reason.

A nine-year-old boy walks into a room where four adults are sitting in a row of chairs facing four empty chairs staged in a square, as if they make up an imaginary car.

Which they were, exactly. That was the point. The read was for the drive-in scene in the pilot episode when Amanda is taking her two sons and another child to get lunch and gets surprised by Scarecrow posing as a pirate waiter.

Walk in. Meet everyone. Shake hands with Kate Jackson. "Ready to do the scene?"

This is forty something year old me talking here, but as I sit and recollect on this time of my life, I can't help but feel this was the perfect moment. I was the right person at the right time. I was prepared. I knew my lines. I knew how to act, how to react. Timing. Wait. Say my lines. Punch my brother, get punched back.

"Who's this man you're whispering to?"

I killed it. You know how I know? Kate Jackson's expression, and that feeling deep inside you when you're having pure fun. That was it for me. Probably the greatest audition I was ever a part of, and later to discover the one that sealed my role on the show. I knew that Kate enjoyed the audition as well. Maybe it was the joy of seeing kids have fun or maybe I really did perform as well as my aging memory recalls. Either way, now it was official...I am Jamie King.

KENTUCKY

"Dear Greg,

...You're <u>really cute!</u>

I wish someday I could see your show live, but for now I'll have to watch you on T.V,"

Molly E.

Somerset, KY

Molly wrote that she was nine at the time of her letter. She had excellent penmanship at her age. Probably the whole women mature faster thing. She included a picture of herself, as well as marking a big red heart with the words "I love you". In a way, I love you back, Molly. That you were a fan and took the time to write is special for me.

But we didn't film our show in front of a live audience, so you coming out to California to watch it live might have been...Weird?

LOUISIANA

"Dear Greg,

...I really enjoy watching the new show "Scarecrow & Mrs. King."

...I've always liked to write to young performers such as, Ricky Schroder, Keith Mitchell, Missy Gold, Glenn Scarpelli, Lara Jill Miller and River Phoenix, just to name a few. "

Michael G.
New Orleans, LA

"Dear Greg,

Howdy there lil bro and I hope you and you family are all doing fine.

...I'm glad you and Paul Strouts are on and I would like to know a little more about y'all.

...I know you have a long and strong career a head and I'm proud to be a fan of yours."

Michael G.
New Orleans, LA

In case you were wondering, it's the same Michael. His first letter is postmarked November of 1983, his second April of 1984. The first was mailed to the CBS studios in New York, which I'm assuming delayed the letter for so long that, in a fit of frustration and discontent, he then mailed another one six months later.

Michael asked a lot of questions that I hope to answer in this book, like how I got started, where I was born, etc. Also, he notes in his first letter that he was a fan of Kate's dating back to her show "The Rookies".

If I'm being honest, when I re-read Michael's first letter, I had to look up a few of the names he mentioned because I didn't know them off-hand. A couple of the faces I recognized, but I'm still not sure who Keith Mitchell is. Keith probably had to look me up too. Regardless, I'll gladly take it anytime someone puts my name in the same class of actor as River Phoenix.

Anyway, I sincerely hope Michael got the autographed picture he had been requesting. I'm sure he did, eventually. After all, he was, apparently, my big bro. Joking aside, let me say this about fan mail. Some people may be insincere in their letters, simply looking to butter me up for an autograph. They may write things they don't truly feel just to get something. Adult me understands all too well those people are out there.

But I'll also say this, over my lifetime I've met a number of fans of my work who are genuinely proud to be fans. True fans. They enjoy the work because it speaks to them, and they are fans of mine because I was a part of it. They want to share that, if even only a little. For those fans, for you, reading this, and for Michael from New Orleans...Thank you.

The FIRST TIME

My earliest recollection of filming Scarecrow and Mrs. King is of me, standing in the kitchen on the soundstage. For the most part, it was a real kitchen. Real sink, real fridge, real counter tops, real food staged inside of real cupboards. The difference was that there was no ceiling, and the backyard was concrete. That, and the thirty or so people standing behind a large camera, all staring at me.

I always notice the lights when I'm on set. I'm not sure why that is, but I think it has something to do with the surreal nature of how those lights create television daylight. The kitchen of the King house was no different. I always noticed the lights. That, and the thirty or so people standing behind a large camera, all staring at me.

In honesty, the first time on the set of a television pilot scared the hell out of me. I had filmed a couple of projects before, but they didn't compare to the scale of a pilot. And that's really it, scale. More sets, more time, more wardrobe, more cast, more people, more lines. Well, actually, lines. I didn't really have lines in my previous work, and uh, well...I had to talk.

For a ten-year-old, all of those people can be intimidating. I've said it twice now, they're all staring at you. It's different on stage. The curtain, maybe? The elevation change between audience and performers? I think the biggest difference between the stage and the set is the casual banter between takes. You don't have that on stage. In theater, there isn't a relationship with the audience outside of the performance. It makes it easier to forget they are there and just do your thing. In theater, your world doesn't extend beyond the edge of the stage.

There are exceptions, of course. When theater actors break the fourth wall and talk to the audience, the stage is nearly meaningless. Plus, the immediacy of the performance is at a higher level on stage. You have one take to get it right. Believe it or not, I prefer those kinds of odds.

I get crazy stage fright before talking in front of people today. Even in front of large groups of people I know well. The first ten to thirty seconds is complete anxiety hell. Heartbeat racing like a turbine, lung function seemingly on vacation, Niagara Falls for palms, light headedness.

Sounds like a bad acid trip. But once I get through that first thirty seconds I'm golden. Beyond thirty seconds, I'm in my element.

But this is adult me writing. Ten year old me didn't realize the thirty second rule (as I'll call it). I had trouble being comfortable on the set. Which, in hindsight, I still don't understand. I was fearless on a stage.

I think it was the mark.

Most people have heard the term "hitting your mark". In film, it refers to your place in the scene, so that the camera can see you and so that you're not blocking fellow actors, either physically or with your shadow. Remember that artificial lighting I was talking about? The lights are set up so that when everyone hits their marks, there are no shadows on people's faces. Shadows are bad for television. It makes it so we can't see the pretty faces.

On stage, you don't really have the same problem. The lights are above the stage directly or projected toward the stage from above the audience. Shadows aren't necessarily an issue because the theater is all about the full body performance. A scene on T.V. can be won or lost on a single raised eyebrow.

What am I saying? That I'm bad at hitting marks? Sort of. At least, there was a learning curve for me. All of the other actors on set were experienced professionals by the time Scarecrow and Mrs. King began filming. Kate and Beverly were Hollywood legends. Paul had done several television shows and a couple of movies before we met. I was the greenhorn. The newb.

To call that pilot episode "The First Time" was appropriate. For all intents and purposes, it was my first time. The film work I had done before paled in comparison. One day shoots were child's play. The minor leagues. This was the big show, baby.

Stay in place. Listen. React. Say my lines. Spread real peanut butter on a sandwich. CUT!!!

No, not the sandwich. The scene. Cut the scene. It's an industry term for stop acting. You've heard it before. As long as it took you to read the above, that's about how quick things move on a set. Maybe not every set, but certainly ours. Like I said, I was dealing with professionals. They don't mess around. They know their stuff.

Picture it this way...I'm a baseball fan. I played Little League one year. You remember, it was that one summer I was playing baseball because I would jump over the ball in soccer? Before this acting thing. So, baseball. Little League. I was nine. Imagine how slow the game moves during a nine-year-old's baseball game. It could take half an hour just for a kid to drag a bat twice his size to the plate for his turn to hit. I'm talking about me, of course. The pitch comes in at what...30 miles per hour?

Now imagine my beloved Cubs. You know, the 2016 World Series Champions? Those guys. Imagine those guys on the field. Sure, they take their signs, survey the field for alignment and strategy. All those things that are the game within the game. Some people may call that slow, but they're all head games. The guys certainly outweigh their own bats. They stroll to the plate. Fidget. Get ready. During my Cubbie's World Series winning run (that'll never get old...for me) they had a pitcher on the team named Aroldis Chapman. He throws the hardest fastball in baseball, clocking in, at times, at 104 miles per hour. One. Oh. Four.

You can't even say one oh four faster than it takes that ball to leave the pitcher's hand and arrive in the catcher's glove. It's like a bullet. For us mere mortals, not blessed with physiques of the gods, hitting a one hundred mile an hour fastball is impossible. For the guys that play in the big leagues, well, it ain't easy. But they can do it. They regularly hit fastballs in the mid-to-high nineties. The game moves fast, but then again, so do the professionals.

That's what it's like to stand on a sound stage in Burbank and have three professionals dance around you during a scene. It goes quick. Sometimes, it was all a little guy like me could do to keep up. Luckily, I didn't have that many lines. Whew...And what lines I had were easy for me to learn. Too easy. Was that what Kate and Beverly and Paul and I had in common, that we had talent and that our lines were easy to learn? Maybe. But what set us apart was that those other three just didn't learn their lines, they also learned everyone else's. They knew where they were in the scene at all times. For them, it wasn't the first time. They had discipline. Me? Not so much.

It drove my mom nuts. Discipline and me didn't really hang out much. Sure, I had raw talent. I still have raw talent. I'm not bragging when I say that, though whenever a guy starts a sentence with "I'm not that guy" well, congratulations buddy, you're that guy! If I didn't have talent, I wouldn't have gotten the part in the show. Or any part. That's why actors get hired, because they have talent. I had it. But I didn't have discipline.

My mom was a dancer in her youth. One of the most valuable lessons she learned as a dancer was practice and the discipline to practice. When I played soccer, I hated practice. When I played baseball? Yep, hated practice. So, why would acting be any different? For me, it wasn't.

I grew up in the eastern San Gabriel Valley, in Claremont. It is a mostly quiet bedroom community. Anyway, Claremont is nearly 40 miles from Burbank, home to Warner Bros. Studios, where we filmed the interior shots for Scarecrow and Mrs. King.

40 miles. In L.A. traffic, that can take about as long to travel as it did for early settlers to move out west. But it's Los Angeles, so think, the Donner Party. In bumper to bumper traffic on the 134 freeway, it isn't uncommon for cannibalism to occur. I kid, of course. Or do I?

It is certainly long enough for a ten, eleven, twelve year old boy with four or five lines maximum per episode to practice his lines in the passenger seat of the car while his mother pressed the gas, and then the brake, and then the gas, and then the brake, and then the gas, and then the brake for half my childhood before arriving at our destination. My mom encouraged it. She knew the value of practice. The value of discipline. She's a good mother! But nope.

"Do you want to practice, honey?"

"I'm okay, I know my lines."

"You know your lines?"

"I know my lines."

"Ok, what are your lines?"

"Why can't Dean take himself to the train station?"

"What?"

"Why can't Dean take himself to the train station?"

"Who is Dean, honey?"

"My mom's boyfriend."

"Oh, that was your line?"

"Uh, huh."

"Was that it?"

"What?"

"Was that all you had?"

"It's not raining."

"It's not raining."

"Uh, huh."

"Why can't Dean take himself to the train station and it's not raining? That's it?"

"Uh, huh."

Frustrating, no? I've never denied I was difficult to live with, even as a child. I was high energy, a dreamer and this, a child who didn't want to practice. Thing is, I did know my lines. Nobody could say I didn't. In fact, it was the one thing I was somewhat paranoid about. Knowing my lines. Talent = 1, Discipline = 0. I told you before I was a little shit.

My lack of discipline never caught up to me filming the pilot. At least, not to my recollection. Twenty years from now Paul Stout will probably write his own memoir with a whole chapter on how his co-star on Scarecrow and Mrs. King was a hot mess. Who am I to say he's wrong?

MARYLAND

"Dear Greg,"

I have seen you on Scarecrow and Mrs. King and I think you are a very good actor.

...Since I am your fan I would also like you to tell me your age and birth date if you don't mind."

Tom R.
Arnold, MD

Tom wanted an autographed picture. He stated he had written a few child actors, and his letter was quite polite. He included a post script *("Thank you very much")* and even a post-post script, mentioning his age and that he was in high school, in case I was wondering.

Adult me was wondering why Tom was asking for both my age and birth date. An obvious attempt at getting me to do his math for him. Ah-ha! You've come to the wrong place, my friend. I'm a writer. We don't do math! We imagine, we infer, we CREATE!

MICHIGAN

"Dear Greg,

Hi! I think you are a fox!

...I am a little taller than you I'm 5' 1".

...P.S. How old are you? And do you like my writing?
Remember always I almost love you.

...P.S. Your Cute and cuddely"

Jennie A.
Edwardsburg, MI

"Dear Greg Morton,

...I saw you on April 2, 1984 at Universal Studios. I
was unable to get your picture and autograph which I
would like very much to have."

Daniella A.
Northville, MI

How Tall Are You?

"Dear Greg,
...I really do think you are cute.
...Do you have any pets?"

Tina G.
Montrose, MI

"Greg,
You must be the cutest kid on the this earth!
...Star Wars is really great. If you think I'm just saying that I'll tell you everything I have.
...Who's your favorite character?
...The Ewoks and Lando Calrissian are kinda unfit for Steven Spielberg's movies I think.
P.S. This is my first letter you, and I hope it won't be my last."

Amy G.
Clakston, MI

How Tall Are You?

"Dear Greg,

...I would also like to know where and how you got your start? Where were you born? Do you have a hobby? What is your favorite food?"

Juanita M.

St. Clair Shores, MI

"Dear Scarecrow and Mrs. King,

I love your show. I watch your show all the time. I really think Greg Morton is cute.

P.S. I'm looking forward to seeing your letter! Please send me a picture of Greg Morton!"

Kelly V.K.

Hudsonville, MI

Jennie, I'm pretty sure, thought I was cute. And cuddely. She did mention she liked my smile, too. She almost loved me. That accounts for something, right? Jennie, I did like your writing. Or rather, I do. At twelve years old, your writing was a very nice cursive, written in red ink.

Daniella had been visiting her grandparents in April of '84, when we missed each other at Universal Studios. I'm sorry that she didn't get a chance for a picture or autograph, and sincerely hoping I sent her something after receiving her letter.

As for Tina's question about pets. I had a pet. A dog. A mutt, spaniel something or other. Cute dog, with long-ish brown hair. Cute, but short. I guess we were the perfect pair. His name was Sugar. *His* name. Sugar. My mom named him. She, my mom, lived in a house with three boys (Dad, Brother and Me), and the male dog got the name Sugar. Mom needed a little girl is what she needed. Anyway, Sugar was a great dog, well loved, and loved well in return.

Amy, I checked, and it turns out I was the cutest kid on Earth. Some kid in Nova Scotia previously held the title. Amy did tell me everything she had for Star Wars, too. Quite an impressive list. To answer her question, I would have to say Han Solo was probably my favorite character, with Chewbacca a close second. And I totally agree that Ewoks and Lando Calrissian are both unfit for Steven Spielberg films, and it's a good thing they never appeared in any.

By the way, I'm pretty sure that *was* the last letter I ever got from Amy.

How Tall Are You?

Of all the cool things I've discovered in these letters, one of the coolest was in Juanita's letter. Still attached is a return address sticker and a twenty-two cent stamp. I fear the stamp is still there because, somehow, a return letter got missed, but I'll hope for the best. Some of the answers to Juanita's questions can be found in this book.

Regarding hobbies, at the time I think playing was my hobby. Swimming and Star Wars were often quoted, as well. My favorite food has changed over the years, as my palate has changed. At the time of her letter (1985) my favorite food was probably hamburgers. Or chimichangas. Now, I fancy sushi, himalayan cuisine, gourmet bar food or anything my wife sets down on the table in front of me. She's an amazing and adventurous cook.

Kelly's letter may be my favorite, though honestly it is difficult to choose only one favorite. I do love that she wrote to the show. Others had done it, and each time I get the biggest kick out of it. I think Kelly's is my favorite because, yes, she's telling the show how cute Greg Morton is. Listen up, people...

PHILLIP, DO NOT HIT YOUR BROTHER in the HEAD with TRASH

Where, exactly, is it okay to hit your brother with trash? I guess maybe this is a question for my own brother, as being the youngest on television and in real life didn't afford me many opportunities to pay it forward. I love this line from the first episode, but have always laughed at it. What she is telling her son is to not throw trash, but what I hear is...Throw trash at another body part. Or hit him in the head with something else. Like a soccer cleat.

Such is my way of thinking. That first episode was certainly the most memorable to film. As I have mentioned before, it was, in most respects, my first time. The drive-in scene was no exception. A location shot. My first real experience with being in front of the camera during a film shoot. It's an odd thing to be on location, especially here in the United States.

When you arrive at the studio, you are arriving to a property that is host to a series of buildings and outdoor set pieces, all behind a secured gate. Just about everyone on the inside is working in one capacity or another, be it cast, crew, executives or support staff. There is the occasional guest or tour, but mostly everyone on a studio lot is in the industry.

What I eventually learned once the pilot became a series, and the series got picked up year after year, is the studio truly becomes your home away from home. The dressing room trailer is in the same location, as is wardrobe and make-up. The commissary, too. At the studio, you are surrounded by these giant buildings. You have your favorite places to stand, to rest, to hide during the day. Just like any other job. You become familiar with walking in and out of the stage door. The red filming light soon fades into the peripheral. You don't ignore it, it just becomes...Common.

That doesn't happen on a location shoot. Not for me, anyway. There are some comforts of home when you're on location. Generally, the dressing room trailer is the same, if not completely familiar. The make-up trailer, too. I'd say hair and make-up trailer, but nobody really messed with my hair. When I first started out, it was Bowl No. 5 for the kid in the chair, please.

Apart from the few familiar trailers set up for the actors, everything else is random and strange. It's a location shoot, out in the real world. One of the strangest parts of the location shoot for me was always arriving to a small army of people invading this one spot, on both sides of the tape that separated fans from the set.

Imagine driving into any small town in America. You're driving down the road surrounded by homes and businesses and lights and trees and whatever else you might see simply driving down the road. All normal, everyday stuff, right?

In the distance? A block or two? It's like a small town has descended on a one acre parcel of earth. As you near, you begin to see equipment trailers, and dressing trailers. People are walking around or milling about. People who are working. And then there are the people who have gathered to watch the people who are working. Plus the lights. Yes, the lights. For exterior shots, that is, for filming outdoors, during the daytime, in daylight, there were a lot of lights. A big bright ball of fire in the sky, and we bring lights to the party. For, you know, extra daylight.

If lights make things a little strange on a soundstage, it makes things downright surreal outdoors. Don't get me wrong, I love the movie magic. I really do. It's just, movie magic is so weird. When you're standing there, looking at these enormous lights pointed at a spot of ground that is already bathed in natural sunlight, you think, this is never going to work. And yet, it does. To perfection. What the audience at home never experiences, though, is the heat. Those lights are hot. As if that big ball of fire isn't hot enough, we raised the dial on the oven.

And it's noticeable. It's like walking through the threshold of a door. Not that when we filmed that exterior shot at the drive-in it was nice and cool outside. It's California. So, that threshold was like going from heat to..."*What the H-E-Double Hockey Sticks??*" I was ten.

Seriously. Being inside the threshold of the lights is like being inside a cocoon of surrealism. Lights, heat, and a world that is supposed to be real, but is just too perfect. The exterior shots were the closest thing to being on stage for me. The soundstage was enclosed. Private. You weren't in a bubble. On location? You're like goldfish. You arrive to this world within a world, retreat to the familiarity of your trailer, get dressed, get made-up, get called to the shoot. You walk through the threshold of reality and make-believe. And all the while, a crowd of people has gathered in the distance, beyond the police barricades.

It's the stage all over again. You are laid bare before the public. You're acting, talking, doing your thing, but in the distance you can see the real world is still out there. Not quite as hot, not quite as perfect. No artificial sun, no hot dogs and sodas that have been sitting for hours. Inside you have a perimeter of space between you and the camera. A moat of reality where anything can be said and heard and done, and it doesn't have to make sense.

That's acting.

I loved every bit of it. Maybe because it's so surreal or because of the movie magic, I'm not sure. Even today I love putting a project together and seeing it through from start to finish. As a child actor, though, I didn't have the responsibilities that others did. In fact, I didn't have any responsibilities. Just enter into the cocoon and pretend I'm someone else, somewhere else, and say my lines. Or ad lib. Like we did in the back of the car at the drive-in.

I did okay in that scene, didn't I? Had one line, said it well. On time, anyway. Got some screen time. Got hit in the head with trash. That was scripted. About five seconds before that, when the food got delivered by an in disguise Scarecrow, and Amanda hands it back to the kids in the backseat? Our lines were not scripted. In truth, nobody wanted the food that was coming back. Not me, not Paul, and not the other kid sitting to my right (whom I cannot for the life of me remember). It was Paul's ad-lib that can be heard in the shot.

"I don't want this!"

If you look closely at my face when Paul says that, what you're seeing is horror. I had no idea what was going on. I thought we wanted that food. I thought we were supposed to take it. We were supposed to be unruly in the backseat, yes. But deny the hot dog? What madness was this? Had I been delivered a different script?

It wouldn't be long before I'd come to expect the unexpected from Paul Stout.

MINNESOTA

"Hi Greg,

...You are a talented actor & it is nice to see you perform.

...Hope to see you in many future projects."

Tom D.
Worthington, MN

"Dear Greg,

...I really admire you and your show. I love to watch it. Sometimes I get mad at my sister when she doesn't want to watch it.

...Do you like Prince?

...What is your favorite movie?

...I really don't know what to write to a TV star! Especially one thats cute like you! Oops! I wasn't going to tell you that! Well, now you know."

Lezlee K.
Hawley, MN

How Tall Are You?

"Dear Greg,

...I have light brown hair and brown eyes too. It sounds like me and you have a lot of things in common except I'm a girl and I don't play with Star wars men! I think you are a real <u>cute boy</u>!

P.S. Please write back in pen Thanks!

Rhonda M.
Foxhome, MN

Tom wanted to see me in many future projects. I hope Tom follows me online. That's the best way to see what projects I'm working on, albeit not all of my work is visual. You know, books and all.

Sometimes I'm mad at Lezlee's sister for not wanting to watch the show too. What's up with that? Lezlee, I do like Prince. I think the term "Genius" is bandied about too often. There are a lot of great musicians out there, but rarely are any of them geniuses. Prince is the exception. He changed music. He changed the music industry. A lot of his music contributes to the soundtrack of my youth.

As far as my favorite movie? Originally Star Wars, for sure. Now? Let's see...How about 180° South by Chris Malloy, featuring Jeff Johnson, Yvon Chouinard and Doug

Tompkins. It's a documentary. That film has impacted me in ways I can't even describe. I highly recommend.

Rhonda had long, run on sentences in her letter, but had incredible penmanship for an eleven year old. It's good that she recognized that, among all of our things in common, I'm not a girl. And let the record show I played with Star Wars toys.

MISSISSIPPI

"*Scarecrow and Mrs. King,*
...I just don't have nothing to say. Sometimes it get
cold, cool and warm down herh."

Lisa B.
Vicksburg, MS

"*Dear Greg,*
I enjoy watching you on Scarcrow and Mrs. King. You
are a good actor as Jamie King. I think you are better
looking than Paul, but he is a good actor too."

Tina T.
Fulton, MS

Lisa sent me a picture of her with friends Mary and Martha. In her letter, she stated that she had sent that same picture to the entire cast, and hoped that we'd return the favor by sending a cast photo to her. I hope she got it. Seriously, anything to make her happy. It can't be easy living in a town that sometimes gets cold, cool and warm. Must be tough to dress for the occasion.

I have been toying with the idea of sending copies of my book to the cast members of the show. Tina has affirmed my decision to send one to Paul, for sure. As I had mentioned before, Paul and I are brothers, and what is more brotherly than sending proof that someone thinks you are better looking?

A RELATIVE SITUATION

If I was hyper and full of energy, Paul Stout was a six pack of Red Bulls after a case of Rockstar. He was kinetic. All the time. To be honest, I'm not sure how he did it. It was exhausting at times to even be in the same room. Don't get me wrong...I love Paul. I love him like a brother. There are good memories and there are not great memories, but I'm not telling you anything I wouldn't tell Paul to his face. I'd be surprised if he didn't know all of this already.

Paul is the oldest of three boys, Ricky and then Scott, the youngest. His mom, Deena, bless her heart, was raising those boys on her own, and they were all three actors. She was a sweetheart, but apparently was a glutton for Hollywood punishment. Having one child actor in the family was more than enough, if you were to ask my mother. Having three must have been quite the task. Like herding cats.

Paul had done some work prior to my meeting him. He had been in the movie Meatballs II with his brother Scott. They played characters named Larry and Barry. Even if he hadn't been a decades old veteran, he still behaved like he knew what he was doing. Which for me was influential, on account of I was clueless to what I was doing, and at any moment someone was going to figure that out. I thought at first I'd take my cues from Paul...Do this, don't do that. But it doesn't really work out that way on set.

It doesn't really work out that way in part because Paul is Paul, and I'm me. I was used to being the center of attention, which in many cases I was, even on the set of Scarecrow and Mrs. King. I used to break dance on the floor of the "family room" on the set, entertaining the crew, in between takes. Just like old times. That was my element. Entertaining. But once the director was satisfied the shot was set up correctly and we were good to go and I was standing on my mark, things changed. Paul was Paul. I was me.

You can't have two hyper kids in one scene, unless the scene specifically called for it. Which, in most cases with us, it didn't. Not that the scene even called for one hyper kid. The script generally just called for kids being kids.

That is basically what they got. I had realized that I couldn't compete with Paul on the energy-on-screen level.

If I'm being honest, sometimes that energy bugged the hell out of me. Not in a professional way, but in a brotherly way. For those four years, Paul was as much my brother as my own biological brother. He taught me, he taunted me, he bugged me and he loved me in return. I think it works on screen, too. There is a real relationship that people are seeing. At times, we might be best of friends and carrying on in the same manner. In hindsight I guess it wasn't that I couldn't *compete* with Paul in energy. I can compete with the Tasmanian Devil in energy. It was whether I wanted to, as his brother. Often, it was a rivalry.

This must be what adult actors feel. A jealousy or paranoia that another actor was outshining them in the scene. We've all heard the stories about co-stars who couldn't get along. Look, Hollywood is a weird, funky business. On the surface, it's superficial. The first thing anyone cares about is looks. Aside from the jack-hammer who is hiring his assistant based on her skirt and not her skills, what business survives on being that superficial? In the real world, it doesn't. Or, at the very least, it shouldn't.

Hollywood isn't the real world.

Except, I never experienced that. Certainly not with Paul. Maybe this is naïveté writing or an adult's failing memory. My relationship with Paul was real. I wasn't jealous of him or his energy on screen. It certainly wasn't paranoia, a feeling I've never experienced. It was that I didn't think his energy was me, or how I wanted to be perceived on screen. For me, the rivalry was - *That is who Paul is...This is who I'm going to be. Let's see who gets more pats on the head.*

I'm like that with my own brother. If my brother was one thing, I was another. Not that I didn't like my brother or didn't love him or even like the things he liked. In some cases, I did. I just didn't outwardly like them because, well, he did. At that age, it's a weird way to compete. I can't speak for Paul, but that was how I viewed my relationship with him. Why? Because we were brothers.

Paul was the unexpected one. If something spontaneous were to happen on screen, it was going to come from Paul. This is most likely due to his experience and his comfort level on set. He was pushing the envelope as an actor, making decisions on screen. I was trying to make my lunch and remember my line and then say it at the point in the scene I was supposed to say it.

That was our relationship on screen. Paul was Paul. I was me.

Off screen? Brothers, through and through. We schooled together, played together, ate together, got into trouble together. I'm sure what our moms really wanted was more sons. They had to co-parent primates. On television. That was a distinct difference, because whether we knew it or not, whether we appreciated it or not, and whether we wanted it or not...Paul and I were, kinda...Brats.

I'll say this, being a child actor isn't the easiest thing to be. We'll discuss it in length later in the book, but for now, just know that growing up is hard enough without being on television. Adding even a modicum of celebrity or privilege to the mix is dangerous. So many stories have come out of Hollywood about former child stars. On some level, I'm one of them. A child star, that is. Not a story. I know, intimately, the struggles. Not with the drugs or money problems, but the psychology. Without the right people in your corner, and I mean people who will fight for you, your mind will easily become FUBAR.

Paul and I are lucky. We aren't tabloid darlings. We had good parenting. That doesn't mean a little snot nosed brattiness didn't creep its way into the mix, now and then. We could be, shall we say, entitled, on occasion. I think I may have told one person at one time..."Do you know who I am?"

UGH.

Yeah, kid. You're nobody. Four feet tall with a head like a bowling ball. That's what I'd say to myself now, if I ever heard those words come out of my mouth. Was Paul ever like that? Sometimes. I don't know if he ever pulled the "Do you know who I am?" routine, but he could be a brat. Maybe he was worse when I wasn't around, but I doubt it. Like I said, we never became tabloid darlings. We did get into trouble, though.

Props aren't magical elements of movie sorcery that come from some hidden alley nobody knows about. They are real objects that come from the real world. They may not always work the same, but they're real. A refrigerator might be a real fridge, but have the back end completely sawed off so that the DP can shove a camera in there and film a little toe-headed kid open up the fridge and pull out a yummy. It may have a gaping hole in it, but it was still once a refrigerator.

On set, the standard kid props were bikes. Which is to say, Paul and I had bikes. Real bikes with real tires, and even real air in them. And those bikes needed to be ridden, because, well, they're bikes. So ride them we did. Often. Kids on bikes. I mean, come on, add some baseball, apple pie and a flag and everyone will start singing 'God Bless America!'

So, Paul and I had these bikes. I don't even remember what kind of bikes they were. BMX, maybe? Boys bikes, anyway. And we'd ride them around the soundstage during break or before lunch or after tutoring. Not far, just around. Except, well, we were on the Warner Bros. lot, and hey, is that the town from Dukes of Hazzard? The front entrance in Hart to Hart? The Walton's House? Gee, it's a beautiful Southern California day, a great day for a bike ride. *Hey Paul...Check this out!*

I'll brag, sure. Why not? I got to tour the Warner Bros. backlot, on my bike, with my brother Paul. Just the two of us, on a perfect day for a ride. Nobody bothering us. Nobody telling us we couldn't run up on the porch or ride on the sidewalk or even in the middle of the street. Nobody telling us what to do.

Nobody knowing where the hell we are...

We were supposed to be on set. Filming. Because, work. The real reason we're there. I don't want to calculate how long we were gone. It wasn't days, for sure. They didn't send Cagney and Lacey or T.J. Hooker looking for us, but I'm sure sending the Equalizer had crossed their minds. Needless to say, two bone-headed boys came rolling back to the sets on our bikes, all casual and happy-like because we'd just had an exclusive look at famous movie and television sets, and soon discovered that we were needed on set.

I wish I could remember the scene we were filming, because you'd probably notice I'm a little light in the backend on that one. My mom was not happy. To put it mildly. She was embarrassed they had to go looking for us, embarrassed that her son wasn't more responsible. I get it. Stupid move. I laugh now, of course. I think maybe if I was the accountant having to pay a bunch of crew to stand around and wait for a couple of runt kids to get back from a joyride I wouldn't be so happy, but then again, I've never wanted to be an accountant.

Maybe it wasn't the smartest thing I've ever done, but it makes for a fun story in my mind. It certainly makes for a fond memory. Of me, and Paul. Brothers. Doing what brothers do. Having fun, and getting into trouble together.

MISSOURI

Dear Greg,
...Are you single?
...I am your kind of girl. I am taller than you.
...My friend Tina is writing too.
To a real Special guy. From a sweet girl.

Joann C.
Hannibal, MO

Dear Greg Morton,
...I think the series is one of the Best series on television today. and that you are a good actor.

Loren G.
Independence, MO

Dear Greg,

...I am a bit bigger then you. But I'm not what you would call short.

...My best friend is writing to.

Tina H.
Hannibal, MO.

Dear Greg,

...I think you and Paul Stout are an important part of the show.

...Do you have any brothers or sisters? You and Paul act so natural as brothers on screen, especially in "The Wrong Way Home" (3rd Season), "Santa's Got a Brand New Bag", and "One Flew East". Those are 3 of my favorite episodes."

Kim W.
Kansas City, MO

Let's talk about Joann and Tina, from Hannibal. Actually, let's first talk about Joann. I wouldn't necessarily categorize a taller girl as exactly my kind of girl. I dated a tall girl once. And by that I mean I followed her around at school for a week, and, upon her not giving me so much as the time of day, I started actually dating a girl who couldn't see the top of my head when we stood next to each other.

Joann, though, professed her like for me, before finally admitting that Tina was going to write, and then she professed her love. Each of the girls warned me the other would write. Warned me. I'll just say that longevity may not have been in the cards for that friendship.

Kim's letter was sweet. In my experiences with Scarecrow and Mrs. King fans, I have found they are most like Kim. Her letter was polite, complimentary, informative about her, and detailed in her memory of the show. When I'm with fans, they are constantly asking if I remember this scene, from that one episode, season such-and-such. That's fandom.

I often feel bad that I don't have the encyclopedic knowledge most fans have. For those of us that worked on the show, the work becomes a blur. Dennis Duckwall, my friend and producer of the show at one time, describes it best when he says the crew's focus was to survive the 7+ days it took to film one episode. Once that episode was done, the focus was on the next 7+ days to shoot. That applies to the actors as well, and in fact might be more appropriate. We have to learn lines, and often have to learn re-writes, in a short period of time for a single story. Before we know it, we have the same process but for a completely different story. I imagine for films the experience is different, but for television, things move pretty quick. Memories aren't what they used to be, either. Thirty five years is a long time.

Still, I'm thankful the fans keep reminding me. It's good to remember.

MONTANA

Dear Greg,
Your pretty cute in the book I have of you.
...How old are you?

Tonya F.
Great Falls, MT

Ok, first...Should I be creeped out there was a book of just me? I mean, that IS what she wrote, correct??

Tonya, I am pretty cute, thank you. Your book is very truthful in that assessment. It must be a textbook. To answer your question, at the time of your letter, postmarked August of 1985, I would have been twelve years old. Twelve and a half, actually. I realize now that book was obviously a picture book, as had it really been a textbook it would have reflected my age at the time. Maybe Tonya just got caught up in my dreamy eyes. Ha ha...Ahem.

The UNIVERSAL STUDIOS MARQUEE

What is the first film you ever remember seeing?

My earliest recollection of film is seeing the original Star Wars out the back window of our car at the drive-in. While everyone else in the family wagon was watching whatever we were there to watch, I was witnessing a silent space battle occur in the distance. Anyone who knows me well knows that I was a huge...HUGE...Star Wars fan growing up. It all began in the back of a car at the drive-in.

That's a testament to the magic of movies, and the wonderful special effects of that movie in particular. Even from a distance, without the proper sound, I was enthralled. Captivated. Hooked. I, like millions of others, have been in love with moving pictures ever since.

My earliest recollection of sitting in a theater to watch a film is, ironically, my mom taking me and my brother to go see the Steven Spielberg classic, E.T. The Extraterrestrial. We didn't know when we went to see the film that later that year I'd be filming my own version of that story for Texas Instruments. At the time, we went to see it because everyone was talking about it. And my mom loves film.

It is a great movie, no question. It's not my favorite science-fiction film, nor is it even my favorite Steven Spielberg film. That honor goes to Close Encounters of the Third Kind. I'm sorry, but you just can't beat Richard Dreyfuss, Teri Garr and Francois Truffaut. And, of course, aliens. Still, I loved E.T. I didn't cry, but I loved it.

That last bit bothered my mom. She still talks about it. She says I have a heart of stone, which, if I'm being honest, more than one person in my life has said to me. I can be...a little cold. Not unsympathetic, though. Or compassionate. I just wasn't emotional over a movie alien. As I get older, that has changed, especially since the passing of my father. Put me in front of Field of Dreams and by the end I'm five and a half feet of blubbering mess.

I will say this, however, that when Elliot has E.T. in his basket on his bike and they begin to fly, I got goose bumps. I may over-use the term 'magic' in this chapter, hell, in this book, but what else can you call it? Spielberg has a way, anyway. For a while, at least, he was Midas with the golden touch. If that man hadn't pursued filmmaking it would be interesting to see what would have become of the movie landscape. There are four faces on the Mount Rushmore of filmmakers and Spielberg is easily one of those immortalized in stone.

And though Walt Disney pioneered the movie/character/television themed amusement park when he opened Disneyland in 1955, no other park identifies itself closer with the *process* of movie making than Universal Studios. Other studios had given tours to guests, but none had created a theme park experience quite like Universal, who began what has evolved into their modern day amusement park way back in 1964.

Living in California since 1979, we, of course, took full advantage of these parks since they were so close to home. It's not often you run across someone who has lived in Southern California for a long time and not visited one or more of the amusement parks located within 100 or so miles of each other. But as I mentioned, none of them get you up close to the process of filmmaking like Universal does.

Needless to say, it was one of my favorite parks, if not *the* favorite. You couldn't go to Disneyland and lift a truck, now could you? All four feet of me acting like a superhero, that'll get my attention. If you've never been, I highly recommend.

So all this is to say that it was incredibly special that in April of 1984 I was invited to participate in Universal Studios' "Hollywood Kids Week". It was a promotion to highlight kids in television and film. This was my first experience with being a celebrity. An amusement park, one that I'd visited countless times as a fan, was to showcase me...As a star!

I knew it was a big deal when, as my mom drove me up Lankershim Blvd. toward the park entrance, I noted the giant marquee out front had my name on it.

I'm still in awe of the magic of filmmaking. Even today, the projects I work on, both in front of and behind the camera draw me in to the process. It's a window of creativity, like a moving diorama. For me, the Universal Studios Tour experience reveals the wonder behind films and television without robbing the process of its magic. Have you ever seen a bad magic show? I have. It is disheartening to see magic not performed well, and leaves you feeling as if you can't believe in magic at all. Thankfully, Universal Studios leaves you wanting more.

My day at Universal began with autographs, pictures and questions. I recently participated in an autograph show, and one fan asked me if I'd done a lot of fan events. I did a fan event at a mall once, with Jeremy Miller from Growing Pains. If I recall correctly, it wasn't like a wave of people had descended on the mall, little girls tugging at their mommies to go see Jamie King, crying. I'm not the Beatles. Or One Direction. That's my memory, anyway. Of the event, I mean. I don't have to rely on memory to know I'm not Harry Styles.

The crux of autograph events is the names. Put me in front of a crowd of people and I can entertain. It's what I do. I'm a dancing monkey. The entertainer is a search and destroy mission, as it were. Search for the funny bone, and destroy it. Get people to laugh, to smile. Tell them a story. Dance like you're on the sidewalk in front of an organ grinder. The sessions aren't just about the communication, though. They're about the memorabilia. The names.

A fan walks up to you, smiles, tells you they're a fan, and asks for an autograph on a picture. They want it personalized. Their name is Lyndah. You write Linda. They just paid you, and now they have an autographed picture that belongs to someone else.

I don't know about Brad Pitt, but that's my nightmare. The names.

Look, I'm all for originality. There are 7 Billion people in this world now, and not everyone is using the same dictionary. There are different names, and there are different ways to spell different names. There are even different reasons for different spellings of different names. Like Nomar. Which is Ramon spelled backward, which is his dad's name. Nomar Garciaparra...This toast is for you!

Former Chicago Cub players, even part-timers like Nomar, get a thumbs up in my book. My book...Get it? I digress.

Look, this isn't 1776. The Declaration of Independence had 6 Johns, 6 Williams, 6 Thomas', 6 Georges, 3 Samuels and a man named Button Gwinnett. That wouldn't happen today. I'm just saying. Not that my personal opinion on names makes any difference. It's still up to the autogapher to ask for, then spell, the autographee's name correctly. Which I learned at Universal Studios that day. Don't assume. Ask Jennifer how she spells her name, and be sure to get it right.

It's J-A-N-N-Y-P-H-I-E-R. It's an old family name.

If you're eleven, a total rookie, and prone to your body working 10x faster than your tiny little mind, you may even spell your own name wrong. Yeah, that happened. So, to say the names freak me out when I'm doing an autograph session is an understatement. Like saying the giant T-Rex looking through the window in Jurassic Park would have freaked us all out is an understatement. So there it is. Names are my T-Rex.

Thankfully, the whole day didn't hinge upon my mastery of the English alphabet or my mom's decision to use four whole letters for my name. After my creative writing session with fan's names, we transitioned to the Screen Test Comedy Theatre shows, which quite honestly was the best part.

The Screen Test was a stage show that invited volunteers on stage to perform in various scenes that showed the audience how such scenes would be choreographed and filmed. The show took volunteers from the audience, paying customers, and brought them on stage to perform in the scene. Once the "actors" took their places, the host or Director would yell *Action!* and the entire scene would be recorded.

The nature of the scenes and the inexperience of the actors would provide comedy gold for everyone involved. Upon ending the scene, the audience was then shown a replay of what was filmed, with all "magic" being hidden from the final product.

My fondest memory of that day was participating with audience volunteers as part of the Screen Test shows. If memory serves, the Screen Test Show put audience members into the role of Keystone Cops for one scene, and in amusement park ride-like articulating bi-planes for another. It was in the bi-plane scene where I helped, as a professional actor, as it were. My role? The Red Baron, the villain of the skies. The bad guy. Sweet, cute, four and a half foot little ole me.

Just remember, I can't spell Lyndah, or at times my own name, so you're not dealing with a Rhodes Scholar here. Which I just realized probably isn't a great attribute for, you know...A writer. Regardless, think kind of me when I tell you these stories. I warned you at the very beginning of this book, I'm prone to making a fool of myself.

There I was, the Red Baron. Badass of the skies. Killer pilot, literally. The scene was set for a dog fight. Me, professional actor against them, rube, amateur citizen audience member. This was it, my big showcase.

Except, well...I couldn't hear. When you're four feet tall, in a bouncing bi-plane staged before a howling wind machine and there is music and laughter and a guy yelling stuff into a microphone it's all a little confusing. That last part, with the guy and the microphone? Yeah, I should have been paying attention to *that* guy. Host. Director of the show. The one guy telling me how to react to the scene, because quite honestly I was having a difficult time seeing anything outside of the plane.

Rule #4 as an actor - Listen to the Director.

In my role as bad guy, I engaged with the heroes in an aerial dog fight. I got shot, however, as previously mentioned I couldn't hear a damn thing, and, well, didn't know I had gotten shot. Instead of raising my fist and scowling at my misfortune, I raised my fist in glee with an ear-to-ear grin in victory. A clever jab by the host about my skills as a "professional" actor and a laugh from the audience later, I realized my error.

Fool.

I guess it's easy to blame the fact that I couldn't hear or even that I could barely see over the steering wheel. I guess, maybe, I shouldn't go on about how I don't consider myself a thespian, that I'm more of an entertainer. Entertain, I did. The crowd laughed, at my expense. As much as I've wanted to be *the* guy, I guess maybe I'm not.

I think back to the days as a kid in our living room with a house full of guests, and me going from person to person telling jokes or stories to get a laugh. Maybe acting, per se, wasn't the right route for me, but it allowed me to do things a great many other people haven't. If it means being a clown on stage and still getting a laugh, I guess that's okay with me. Even if it was my "day".

NEBRASKA

Hi Paul Morton

...I want a picture of yourself please

> *Debbie B.*
> *Seward, NB*

Dear Greg,

...And also you are good look.

> *Elizabeth B.*
> *Seward, NB*

Debbie and Elizabeth shared a last name, but the return addresses, though both in Seward, were different. Cousins, maybe? They must have shared a penchant for tiny notes, as each letter was written on paper that was then cut to roughly 5" square.

How Tall Are You?

To be honest, I'm not sure how I got Debbie's letter. The folks at CBS (where the letter was mailed to) must have Rock/Paper/Scissored the destination, as the envelope, too, was addressed to Paul Morton.

NEW JERSEY

Dear Greg,

...You are so cute, do you think I could get a personalized photograph of you?

...I'm going to be 12 March 7th, 1974, and I'm 4" 10"...

...And I'm single too.

P.S. ...I'm in the 5th grad and have 3 boyfriends, here are their names...

Brian -

John -

Greg Morton (you)

Love your #1 Fan
Cynthia C.
Franklin, NJ

Dear Greg,

...I know you must be asked this constantly, but can we be pen pals?

Love ya,
Robin D.
Bloomfield, NJ

Dear Greg Morton,
I think you are really cute.
...My friend Nancy and I think you are really cute.

Love ya,
Gina S.
Bloomfield, NJ

I've never been to New Jersey, but Jersey girls loved me apparently. I guess I've been missing out.

Let's get a few things straight, though. Cynthia was blinded by love. She was single, but with boyfriends Brian and John and a *wish-list* because, as I mentioned, I've never been to Jersey. And, at four inches ten inches tall, she was probably still too tall for me. I wonder what ever happened to Brian and John, honestly.

How Tall Are You?

I think Robin was the first to ask if we could be pen pals. If not the first, certainly one of the very few.

Gina thought I was cute and wrote me a letter. Nancy thought I was cute, but didn't write.

I'm just sayin'...

NEVER LOOK a GIFT HORSE in the MOUTH

I was dressed up like a tree.

It was the first time I had ever worn tights. I think maybe the last time, too, but I did have a "girlfriend" in Junior High that liked to dress me up. It wasn't as fun as it sounds. The quotes, as they are, indicate she wasn't really my girlfriend. Dressing me up was, apparently, her way of torturing me? I'm not sure. I liked her, she didn't like me, it's Halloween, here, put on this dress. I digress.

I was dressed up like a tree. It was the sixth episode of the first season, and, needless to say my pride was a little...Damaged. It wasn't comfortable, I thought I looked ridiculous, and they had at one point attached fishing line to my costume so that, at the right time, they could pull leaves off of me. I'm green, literally, and they are tugging on me with fishing wire. Not my best day for self-esteem.

How Tall Are You?

Put me in a green costume today and tug on my leaves and I'd be a happy man. Wait. Is it just late or did that not sound right? Regardless, there were times I didn't really appreciate what was happening to me as an actor. Being dressed up like a tree was one of those occasions. Looking back is bittersweet. I wish I had known better.

Hindsight is 20/20. If I could go back and do things again, I'd do them mostly the same, but different. How was I supposed to know, at ten, that what I was doing was special? My parents, bless their hearts, did an amazing job at keeping me grounded. For the most part. As high energy and eager to entertain as I was, I wasn't some out of control ego-maniac. I had my moments of confusion. And confusion was really what it was.

Most of our scenes were in the living room or kitchen, and as I've mentioned before, I was typecast as a super cute little boy. This was life, for me. I'll talk about, and have discussed already, that this show and the cast and crew were like family. They cared for me, joked with me, talked with me. Paul and I had our brother thing going. We spent most of our time in one "house". Family.

For a kid whose imagination was bursting at the seams, it was too much normal. In my mind, I wanted to go places, do things, be...Someone other than a cute, lovable, cute little boy. Yeah, I wrote cute twice.

Don't get me wrong, at no point did I hate being on the show. Never. I loved it, and especially now, I appreciate not only the opportunity it was, but the gift it continues to be for the fans. But I'd be totally lying to you if I said that it was all roses for me at the time. It wasn't.

And I blame youth.

More specifically, I blame the fact that I was a child actor. Look, growing up is hard. Just being a normal *I play, I school, I play, I sleep kid* is difficult. Growing up is sensory overload. Everything is a learning experience, both internal and external. I've written about this before in my book Lifting a Foot Forward that, as children, our lives are dynamic because everything is new. Each day is a day for discovery. That book touches on this perspective for adults as a means of having a balanced life, to challenge ourselves each day. To push ourselves outside of our comfort zone. To help us get back to a dynamic life.

One problem. As a child, you don't realize you're living a dynamic life unless you live in a commune, wear a lot of linen and smell like a campfire. Or unless your parents are forward thinkers who communicate with you. Whichever.

My point is that I had all of this creative energy inside of me, and even though I had an outlet for some of it, I didn't have an outlet for all of it. Rather, I didn't recognize I had an outlet. Reflecting back, I would have continued to do school theater or started a band or learned to paint. Most of all, I wouldn't have been embarrassed to be a tree.

NEW MEXICO

Dear Greg,

We have a lot of things in comin

1.   We are both 4'4"

...On T.V. there are two boys that I think are cute!!
They are RICKY Sroder + GREG Morton!

...Please write me a letter...

...and if you can get Michael Night the star in Night
Rider's address I will be thrilled!

Anna B.
Cerillos, NM

Anna's letter was adorned with various stickers, including a break dancing sticker she wouldn't even give her boyfriend or so she declared. I found it funny that she listed my height, eye color, hair color and the fact that I enjoyed swimming, but didn't know my age. There was apparently a limited amount of ink available for the TV Superstars Scrapbook.

Anna also wanted my home address so that she could write me more. I'm thinking between Ricky Sroder, Michael Night and her boyfriend Mark, Anna didn't really need me in the mix.

NEW YORK

Dear Greg,

Why don't you appear on Scarecrow and Mrs. King alot?

Nicole A.
Pleasant Valley, NY

Dear Greg,

We wanted to write to tell you that we enjoy your portrayal of Jamie on "Scarecrow and Mrs. King".

Marilyn + Marion C.
Bellerose, NY

How Tall Are You?

Dear Greg,

...I'm one of your biggest fans. I watch Scarecrow and Mrs. King every Monday night. I really like the show a lot.

...Which one do you play on the show?

Your Fan,
Donna D.
Jamestown, NY

Dear Mr. Morton,

I am starting a collection of signed photographs of outstanding actors. It is therefore in deep humility that I make this request for a signed photograph of yourself to add to my collection.

Joseph F.
Brooklyn, NY

Greg Morton,

...Please tell me, what other television programs and movies have you been in besides SCARECROW AND MRS, KING ?

Kelly K.

APO, NY

Dear Greg,

...You are cute + a good actor. Would you please tell me some about yourself?

Faye K.
Binghamton, NY

29 OCT 1985
To CRAIG MORTON
I SENT A LETTER TO GET A AUTOGRAPH
PICTURE FROM YOU I WATCH YOU ON SCARECROW
AND MRS KiNG Did You START ON ANY oTher
SERIES...

3 DEC 1985
To GREG MORTON
I Would Like To Know iF I Could A Autograph
Picture From You I Watch You On SCARECROW AND
MRS KING Did You Start On Any oTher SERIES...

9 JAN 1986
TO GREG MORTON
I Would Like to Know...

LIVE LONG AND PROSPER
William L.

LIC, NY

10 JAN 1986

Dear Greg,

...I am eleven years old and my favorite television show is Scarecrow and Mrs. King (and I'm not just saying that, because it <u>is</u> true.)

29 JAN 1986

Dear Greg,

Do you enjoy being on a popular television show?

...What is your favorite sport?

Lisa M.

Altamont, NY

Honestly, Nicole, I asked myself that question all the time. All joking and selfishness aside, I think from a story standpoint the kids were underutilized as a source of good material. Amanda was juggling life as a mother and international spy. That had to have an impact on her kids. It would have been cool to explore that more.

Marilyn and Marion sent a handwritten letter on a piece of paper measuring 2-5/8" wide by 4" long. Grab a ruler right now and see for yourself what that looks like. Go ahead...I'll wait.

Tiny, right? They wrote the date, a salutation, five sentences and their names and address all on this tiny little slip of paper. The envelope is literally three times bigger than the note that was inside.

One of those sentences mentioned they enjoyed the Christmas episodes the best. This was reinforced by their use of a Christmas stamp, two additional Christmas stamps on the back of the envelope and a Christmas themed return address sticker. Their letter was postmarked January 5th, so I'm guessing the girls wanted to write to some obscure ten year old on T.V. and their mother made them use the leftover stamps from all the Christmas cards they sent out.

Donna D. watched our show every Monday night, was one of my biggest fans, and had no idea which of the two brothers I played on the show. I think that sums up my career nicely. To answer Donna's question...I played the short one.

Joseph in Brooklyn wrote arguably the most formal and polite autograph request letter I've ever read. Handwritten, of course.

How Tall Are You?

Kelly typed her letter, but signed it. Scarecrow and Mrs. King was the only television show I've ever done, but I did do a made for TV movie once, and a photograph of me and Paul Stout appears in the movie Lethal Weapon 3, the least lethal of all the Lethal Weapon movies, in my opinion.

Faye, when I was a teenager I enjoyed eating pretzels and orange juice together.

William in Long Island City (or LIC, for short) wrote three letters, each letter was two pages and each was one long sentence that lacked anything resembling punctuation. Remember Joseph in Florida? He was matched in persistence by William for sure. I'm not entirely sure if over the years his letters have gotten mixed with their correct envelopes or if William really did begin his first letter telling me he had sent me a letter. We'll never know.

New Yorkers like William and Lisa M. must have been getting some serious snow in December 1985/January 1986 to write so many letters so close together.

Lisa, my favorite sport is baseball, but I enjoy nearly all things sporting. As a kid I enjoyed skateboarding the most, and am still drawn to it (though I don't skate as much as I used to). Now I'm either hiking or surfing for sport, but I'll still watch baseball during the summer.

Lately, I've been watching Curling Night in America on television. I wouldn't say that I'm a fan of the sport necessarily, but I am finding it interesting to learn about something new. And who doesn't love a sport where a broom is part of the equipment?

How Tall Are You?

Top Left: 1975 me. Peak super-hero cuteness. Everything about my face has been downhill since.

Top Right: Me, my dad & brother at Universal Studios (pre-acting days). My expression is proof I'm a ham when there's a camera pointed at me. Also, when you're this short, every sock is a knee high.

Top Left: #12. Evidence I played soccer, and the only time I wasn't jumping over the ball.

Right: My one and only baseball picture. I'm pretty sure the bat was taller than me by about 3 or 4 inches.

How Tall Are You?

Spring Sing, 1982 - My first time performing on a real stage
and I got a solo. I was hooked!

Top: Summer of 1982 - I'm the fifth orphan from the left in the
Mickey Rooney's Talent Town Production of Oliver!

Right: Performing a solo of
"I Won't Grow Up"
at the Los Angeles County Fair,
August, 1982.

My first professional head-shots.

You know it's Hollywood when a nine year old boy with hobbit
ears poking out of his helmet hair is wearing a plaid button down
collared shirt and posing with his arms crossed and the picture
just screams "Hire Me!"
(Or I'll fight you...See bottom left image.)

My brother Jeff, Kate Jackson and Me.
Burbank Studios Backlot, 1983.

How Tall Are You?

Me, Kate and Paul.

Paul, Bruce and Me.

On Location in Burbank, CA

Right: Paul Stout
photobombing me
in the wardrobe
trailer

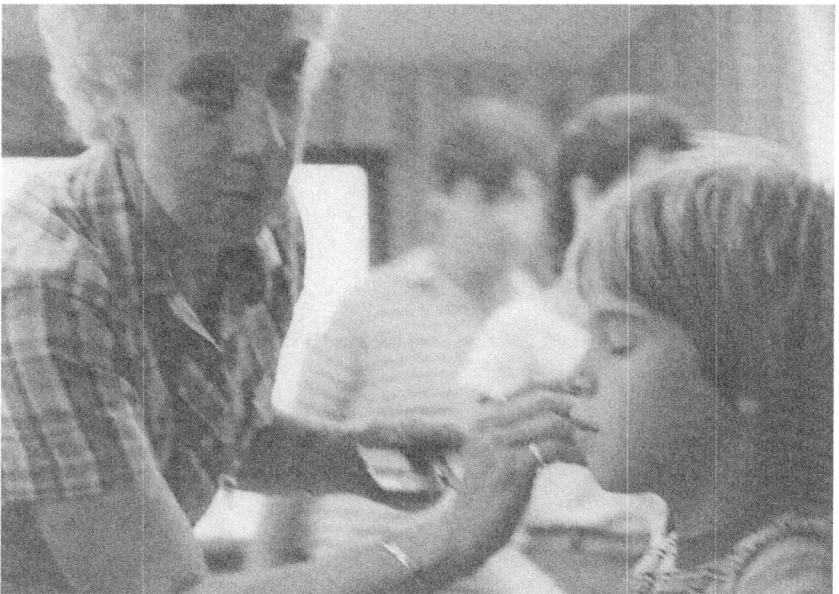

In the hair and make-up trailer with Hollywood Icon
Beverly Garland to my left.

How Tall Are You?

You're a huge star when they put your name on your trailer with masking tape. Masking tape, baby!!!

Also, I like crossing my legs when I pose.

How Tall Are You?

Yes, I like posing in doorways.

Yes, my legs are crossed.

No, you didn't believe me.

Also, This was where Paul and I had to do our
required schooling when we worked.

In a metal box.

With no windows.

And all my teachers wondered why I hated school...

How Tall Are You?

The chairs are not a myth.

Most people get tall studio chairs. Mine was a little closer to the ground. Also, please notice it's disheveled. And dirty.

Me and Bruce Boxleitner

Burbank Studios, 1984

The only time Bruce and I have ever been the same height.

How Tall Are You?

My name in lights.

Star of the Day at Universal Studios.

April, 1984

Cast party with Martha Smith.

On location in Germany with Mel Stewart.

How Tall Are You?

Paul and I being escorted to the set on location in
Munich, Germany. Summer, 1984

Filming a scene for the episode
"The Times They Are a Changin'"
Munich, Germany

How Tall Are You?

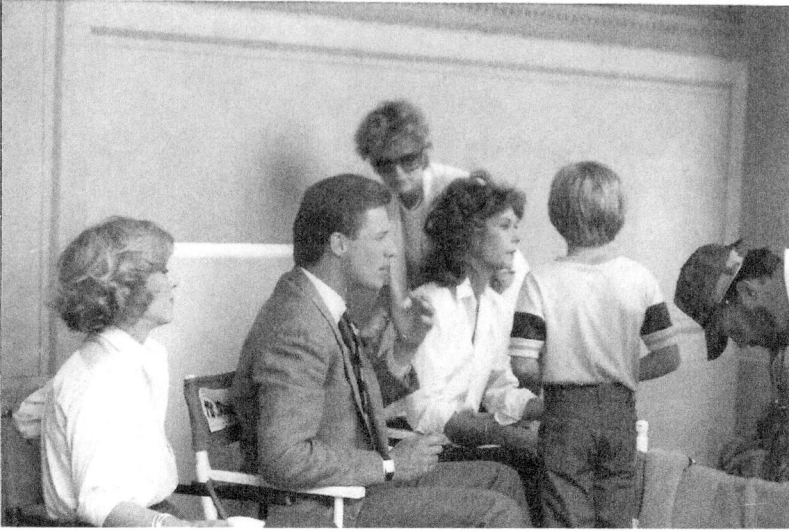

My mom, God bless her. This would have been a perfect "Behind the Scenes" photo of the cast, except for the monkey with his back turned. To set the record straight, my mom is taking a photo of Bruce. Not her son.

The two crew people in this photo are Kate's hair and make- up artists. They were such awesome people. I spent a lot of time with them on set.

DISCLAIMER

Remember, this was the '80s. It was not a time everyone had a high quality phone/camera in their pocket. As such, we took more SMK photos in Germany than we did back home because we were on vacation. I mean work.

I guess this didn't really need a disclaimer. But there it is.

Filming in Munich. You can't kick the locals out of your filming location, you can only rope them off. And hope they don't stare right into the camera. But they do.

They always do.

Bruce gets his picture taken a lot because he's pretty. And because he's pretty cool.

My mom here (striped shirt) is rocking some serious 80's style. Also, notice her close proximity to *You-Know-Who?*

Bruce with his stunt double. Munich, Germany

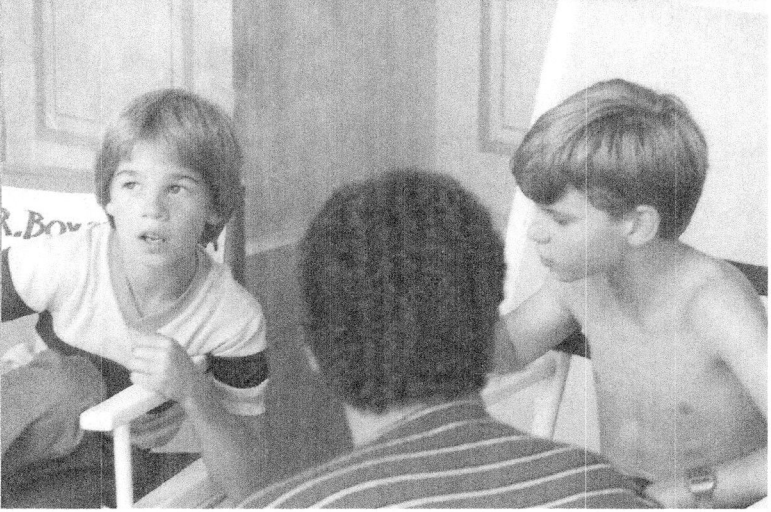

Brothers.

Jamie and Phillip.

This is one of my favorite pictures of me and Paul.

How Tall Are You?

Me, my brother Jeff, Paul and his brother Scott.
Oberammergau, Germany.

Adventurers in a foreign land.

This cool cat is my dad. Rocking the SMK hat, ever proud of his son. My mom took a lot of pictures of him, too. She thought he was the coolest. Take that, Bruce whatever your name is!

My entourage. They go everywhere with me.
Always. I love these people.

Grandma & Mom

Beverly Garland and Kate Jackson

Me photographing Beverly and Kate on set in Munich.

How Tall Are You?

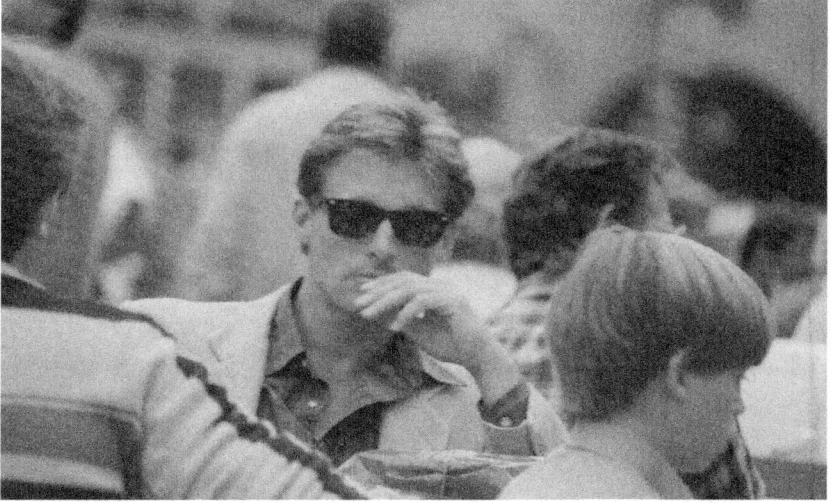

"The Picture"
Bruce Boxleitner on the Marienplatz, Munich, 1984.

Bruce talking out a scene on set while
my dad and brother look on.

How Tall Are You?

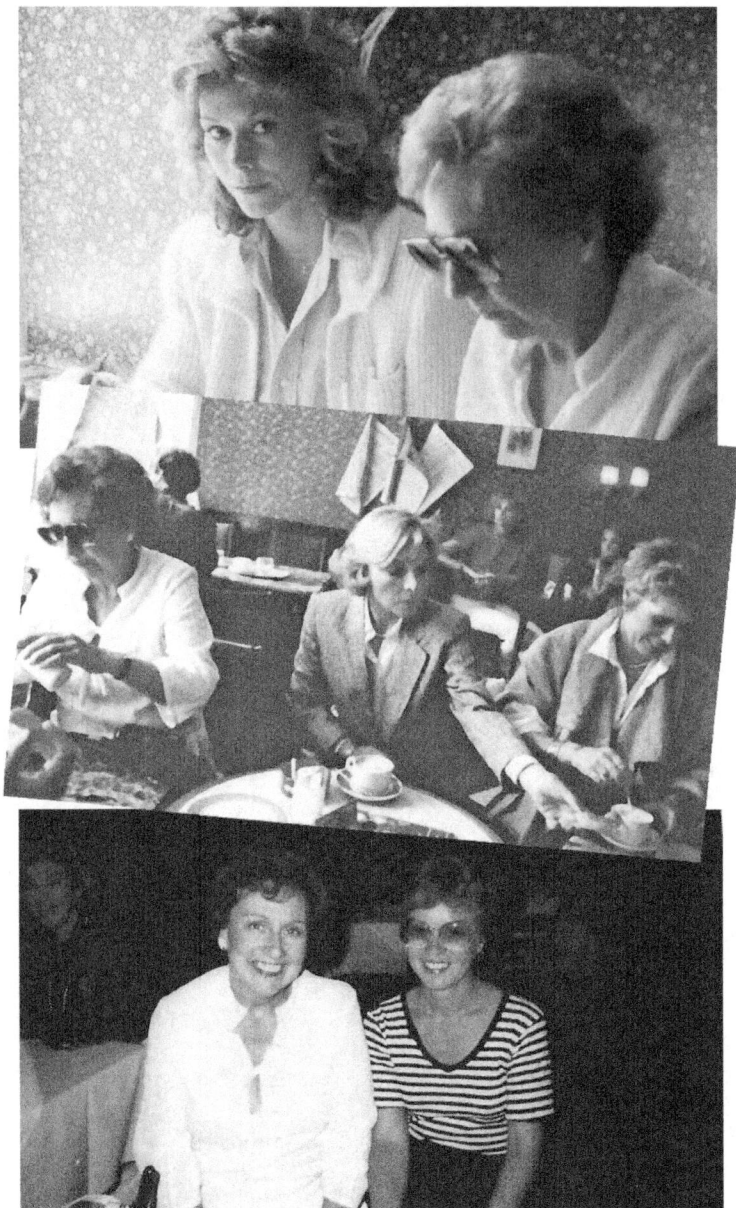

Private Lunch with Kate, Beverly, and the incomparable Jean Stapleton. Everyone getting in on the picture action but yours truly. Not that I'm bitter. As a small consolation to my fragile ego, it helps to know I took these pictures.

Opening Christmas gifts in Kate's trailer, Burbank Studios, 1984. I'm sitting between Beverly to my left and my Grandma Heller to my right.

Oblivious to anything around me but gifts.

My brother Jeff, Beverly Garland and Me.
Christmas Party, Burbank Studios, 1984.

Last one from Germany. I love this picture.

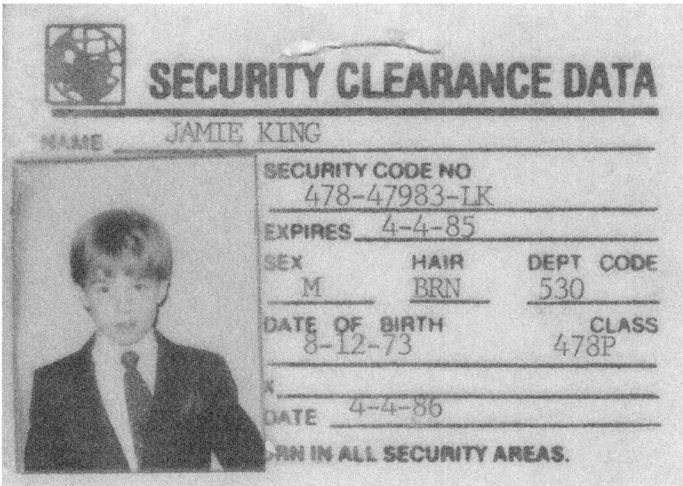

Pocket square and all. That's how agents roll.
This is the only prop I kept from actual filming.

My apologizes to Andrea Barber for this picture. It's
the only one I have of the two of us, and her eyes are
closed. At least she can't see how enormous my head is.

Sal Mineo's wetsuit. I'm sure it was a priceless artifact that some kook ended up wearing in his pool.

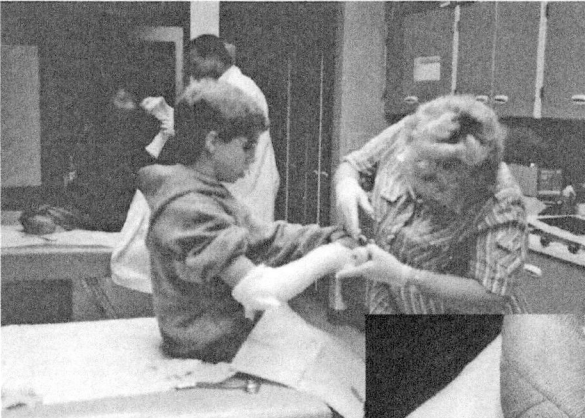

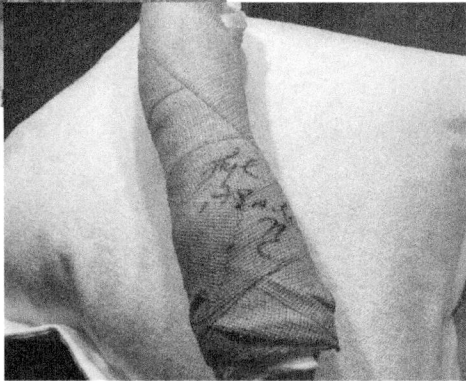

This nurse had no idea how precious, and valuable, this cast would be.

Lyle Alzado's autograph still stands alone.

Admittedly, this isn't the best, most flattering picture of me or my mom. But it tells the whole story. I get my kook from her. This kind of crazy happens every time we're together.

Thanks, mom, for all you've done and all you do. The managing, the chauffeurring, the care-taking, the shooing, and everything else you did for my career that I'm sure I've forgotten about and won't give you credit for in person.

I love you.

How Tall Are You?

L-R - Me, Martha, Bruce (in back), Dennis Duckwall, Myron Natwick and Stephen Macht.

The Hollywood Show

2017

Me in front of the original King home filming location in Burbank, CA. 2016

My wife and I on the set of Friends, Warners Bros.
Studios, 2017

I've learned a lot about myself over the years. Not all
of it good. I've learned being a child actor affected me in
ways I didn't realize. I haven't always been easy to live
with.

What I've learned about myself, I've learned because I
have a smart, strong woman who loves me, and who
challenges me to be a better person.

I would say more, but I need to keep the really soft
and mushy stuff for when I've done something stupid and
I need for her to remember she loves me.

And to kiss my face.

LAS VEGAS and the JERRY LEWIS TELETHON

Growing up, Labor Day weekend meant two things. First, school was to start soon. Not something kids look forward to. Is it possible to despise a holiday? Is it appropriate to despise a holiday dedicated to work? Anyway, Labor Day weekend also meant the Jerry Lewis Telethon (as we commonly called it) aired live on television. The Muscular Dystrophy Association helped organize and televise this annual event, with Jerry Lewis its founder and host from 1966 until 2010.

Every year the Telethon was an event in my house. As my brother and I got older, the challenge became how long we could watch continuously, as the show historically ran for 21 or so hours between Sunday and Monday each Labor Day. I have some of my earliest recollections watching famous Hollywood talent from this program on television each year.

How Tall Are You?

In 1986 I was honored to be invited to participate as a celebrity answering phones, at the center of the Telethon universe, Las Vegas. This was a big deal, mind you, as the Telethon operated satellite locations across the country for the broadcast. I could have been invited to travel all the way to the exotic locale of downtown Los Angeles! Instead, knowing what a huge celebrity I was, I'm sure, they just had to have little ole me at the big show. For me and my family, this was akin to being invited to the White House. Imagine it, me, asked to be on stage with Jerry Lewis!

Let me give you a little background on this whole celebrity thing. This isn't something I take all that seriously, to be honest. That's not to say I don't respect my accomplishments as a working actor or disregard where I've been or what I've seen. I very much respect those things. This book is a living testament to that respect, as one goal is to help highlight and remind myself that I have had some impact on the lives of others through this experience of being a "celebrity".

But what does "celebrity" really mean for a guy like me? I'm just a regular guy with some pretty special experiences. Let's face it, nobody is thinking "Whatever happened to that cute little helmet haired kid from Scarecrow and Mrs. King? His acting really moved me."

If there is an alphabetical list to gauge the level of celebrity, I'm sure my name ranks somewhere down near the last vowel. I'll boast my integrity as a celebrity surpasses that of a reality star, but that's about it. I'm not about to step into a boxing ring with that girl robot from Small Wonder. Or live in some house with an aged rap star, scream queen, celebrity criminal, fringe comic and circus freak like it's a Bizzaro World version of Clue. I might dance, though, if they had a "Where are They Now" special of Dancing with the Almost Stars. *I got da moves.*

When I was on television, it was primarily work. I was having fun, but I was too young to be out on the town, soaking up the riches of my celebrity. I was home, like any other kid my age, struggling with school work or fighting with my brother or trying to con my parents out of more dessert. I can guarantee you, Tiger Beat magazine never snapped a candid of me walking out of a Baskin Robbins.

My junior varsity celebrity status was one of the reasons something like the Jerry Lewis Telethon was so special. It was like being a part of an elite club. In the grand scheme of things, how many people got asked to do something like that? How many got asked to participate in Las Vegas? It was like being invited to the adult's table at Thanksgiving, but still being so short and so young that your feet swung off the end of the chair. I was just so excited to be there, I didn't know what to do with myself. Like looking in on the real celebrities, and then having them ask you inside for a drink.

No, really. I didn't know what to do with myself when I got on stage. Ever look back on a photo that was taken of you, and you can't quite remember what the heck was going on in your mind when the picture was snapped? That is my memory of walking out on stage at the Telethon.

Look, I've said it before, my memory isn't great. I'm probably not the best candidate for a memoir, if I'm being honest. Of course, those who would agree with me never got this far into the book to witness my admission of guilt. Their loss, I guess. It's tough to remember stuff that happened thirty years ago, when you were a kid, and amazing things were happening to you. Like shock and awe.

Some things, however, stick with you for a lifetime.

My dad taught me how to tie a necktie that weekend. It's not too often that you could pin down the date of an event as unassuming as when your dad taught you how to tie a necktie. Normally, we lose those kinds of moments. Or maybe we remember them, but can't remember when they happened. You often hear things like "I think I was five or six when that happened. Maybe seven?" For me, I can pin down a memory to Sunday, August 31st, 1986. A good memory in the hotel, in front of the mirror, having a legendary father/son moment. Tying a tie.

"The rabbit ran around the tree..."
"Under the bushes..."
"Over the log..."

Basically, my greatest memory of appearing on the world famous Jerry Lewis Labor Day Telethon was time spent with my family.

I did meet other celebrities, though. I met Emmanuel Lewis, from the hit show "Webster", in the lobby of the hotel. That kid was everything you'd expect him to be. Funny and nice. He gave me the impression that he really appreciated the celebrity he enjoyed, not because it fed his ego, but because it meant success for him as an actor, and I think more importantly he enjoyed the conversations with fans. And I also met...Ok, I can't remember. I'm sure I did meet celebrities, plural, but Webster maxes out my recall.

The point of the trip was the Telethon. Remember I wrote earlier that I didn't know what to do with myself when I got called onstage? Yeah, so, when they called my name, I emerged from the darkness offstage, threw up my hands for a double wave like I was Nixon (thankfully no peace signs) and then stepped stage right to the panel of celebrities answering phones. A double wave. A four foot tall, top-heavy, quasi-celebrity in a grey double breasted suit and newly learned-how-to-tie necktie tossing out the double wave. Let that sink in for a moment.

I'll be honest, I wish I still had video. I've looked on the inter-webs but can't find it. Nothing would please me more than to see the double wave. Again.

My biggest question leading up to the Telethon was "Are celebrities answering real phones?" The answer? Yes. And it was incredibly hard to hear anyone on the other line. You're trying to conduct business on stage while the host is encouraging others to sing, dance and tell jokes ten feet from where you're sitting. You know, entertainment. You want a taste of the experience? Head to the nearest Chuck E. Cheese's restaurant (or similarly themed food/playground establishment). Plant yourself in the middle of the arcade. Turn the volume down on your cellphone so that it's one bar away from mute. Now make a phone call. To the oldest, most soft spoken person you know.

I could have been taking pizza delivery orders, for all I know. As has been the case more than a few times in my life, I'm confident I didn't do a great job of being "Celebrity Phone Guy". I can only imagine the sheer disappointment of the philanthropist on the other end of the phone, hoping to speak to someone they'd actually heard of and got the voice of puberty on the line. If you called me that night, I'm sorry. If I ever become, like, actually famous, you can call me and we can chat.

At least your money went to a good cause.

I was 13 at the time. I was a little overwhelmed and hadn't yet learned the art of enjoying the moment. It was also one of the first times, if not *the* first time, I remember feeling small. Not belittled, but just that the world around us sometimes has a way of reminding us how big it can be. That stage. Those lights. I'm sure the A-Listers don't quite feel the same way, but to a kid, that world can be immense.

Oh, and I wasn't introduced onstage by Jerry Lewis. The man was hosting a twenty one hour television marathon, he wasn't going to stand onstage the entire time yelling "Hey Lady"! It was 1986. This was pre-Red Bull. No, Jerry Lewis was backstage. Resting. I got Ed McMahon. Not quite the legendary comic and headliner of the show calling me out on stage, but...If Ed was good enough for Johnny, then he was good enough for me.

NORTH CAROLINA

Dear Greg,

Hi! My name is Euva. I am 9 years old.

...Well...enough about me. Let's talk.

...I wish you were the leading actor on "Scarecrow and Mrs. King." When you are in it I just faint.

Euva H.

Forest City, NC

Everyone has a story to tell. Euva told me her name, age, grade and school. Well, enough about her. She thought I was cute and fainted when I was on her television. Let's talk about *that*!

OHIO

Hi! Greg,
Your so <u>cute</u>!

Angie B.
Clarksburg, OH

Dear Greg,
...Always one of a kind.

Garland C.
Dayton, OH

Dear Mr. Morton,
Hello. I saw you in one of my books I have.
...Singe, Mrs. Kathy D.
P.S. You will write bake won't you? Oh sorry how
old are you. I'm 13 and has trouble spelling.

Singe,
Mrs. Kathy D.
Bryan, OH

How Tall Are You?

Dear Greg,

...You are a talented young actor.

...I want you to know God loves you.

> *Melody D.*
> *Bloomingdale, OH*

Dear Greg, Your cute!

...Do you have a girlfriend?

...Would you please write back telling me the answers to the questions above?

> *Heather E.*
> *West Unity, OH*

Dear the cuty (Greg)

I like the show "Scarecrow and Mrs. King". The best shows are when you are on alot.

> *Jennifer K.*
> *Bethel, OH*

31 JAN 1985

Dear Greg,

Hi. I'm a fan of Scarecrow and Mrs. King. You are great a James.

22 FEB 1985

Dear Greg,

Hi, I'm a fan of Scarecrow and Mrs. King. You are great as James King.

Joan O.

Kettering, OH

Dear Greg,

...I really like watching you on the show and I would like to know if you could send me an autographed picture.

Peggy P.

Bellecenter, OH

OCT 1984

Dear Gentlemen,

...A lot of shows don't make sense but in this one I always know what is going on, and there isn't alot of dumb kissing, either!!

...Last month I asked for a picture of Greg Morton, who does a great job on his part.

...My reason for writing is really to ask for a picture of Greg Morton.

21 DEC 1984

Dear Greg,

...When are the writers going to put you guys in some of the "adventures"? Now <u>that</u> is worth an hour (or 2) show!

...You probably get bags of mail every week from other kids wanting your picture, I bet. And especially from girls. I feel sorry for you 'cause the ones in my grade tell me I'm "cute" and follow me + my friends around. How you and Paul stand it is beyond me!!

...You ought to drop some hints to the writers about REALLY letting you guys show your talent on the show, okay?

Chris S.

College Corner, OH

12 SEP 1985

Dear Greg,

...Also, I'd sure like a picture of you, Greg. Already have one from Paul Stout + Kate Jackson.

Chris S.

Oxford, OH

How Tall Are You?

Dear Mr. Morton,

...You are a great actor! They always give you and Paul Stout funny things to say and do! You are both really funny!

Russ W.
Glenmont, OH

Angie's letter was simple and direct, with a plain sticker on the back that she handwrote the word "fan". In case it wasn't clear. Garland's letter was a greeting, three short sentences and a salutation. She left a full two thirds of page blank, but at least she sent a full sized sheet.

I'm curious if 13 year old Kathy D's parents knew she was addressing herself as Mrs. There was no doubt that girl was ready for marriage. Probably had her dress picked out.

God loves me. I know She does. Thanks, Melody.

Heather asked a number of questions, and I surmised the most important of which was if I had a girlfriend. Her letter was postmarked November of 1985, so, no. I did not have a girlfriend. In 1985 I may have been cute on television, but in real life no girl ever said that to me.

I agree with Jennifer that the best shows were the ones I was on a lot. But then again, I may be a bit biased.

I have to be honest, one thing that has always puzzled me was the names of the characters on the show. Amanda, Dotty, Lee, Billy, Francine, Phillip and Jamie. I've wondered what inspired those exact names. It's clear Joan had her own opinions on the subject.

Peggy, I really liked being watched on the, er...uh. Maybe this isn't going to sound as funny as I'd like. How about, Peggy, I really liked being on the show? Not so creepy? Great!

Chris in Oxford is the same Chris from College Corner. He wrote a year after sending his first two letters, and mentioned that he had moved. It seems as though he never got a photo from me, at least, not as of the twelfth of September, 1985. If it's true he never got a picture; that saddens me more than you can imagine. His letters were handwritten, of some length, funny and complimentary. And he wrote three, certainly deserving of reciprocity.

Paul and I were kids, playing kid roles, doing kid things. That resonated with Russ. Selfishly, I assume after a while kids continued to sit with their parents and watch the show because they wanted to see Phillip and Jamie. For many my age, including myself, a lot of the spy elements went over our heads, but it was the relationships that kept us engaged. The banter between Amanda and Lee, Amanda and Dotty, Lee and Francine, Phillip and Jamie.

I think, still, the show continues to resonate in people's lives because of those relationships onscreen.

REMEMBRANCE of THINGS PAST

Let's just say I had a love affair with Kate Jackson, and leave it at that.

Not a romantic affair, mind you, as I was a child. But a love affair, nonetheless. To this day, she holds a special place in my heart. And why wouldn't she? For four years I was her youngest child, and quite honestly, she treated me as such. Maybe the years have been kind to my memory, but if so, I'm okay with keeping it that way.

I come from a very small family. Immediately there were four of us. My brother and me, my mom and my dad. My mom is an only child, and my maternal grandfather passed away before I was born. My dad was one of four in his family, but they all lived in Illinois. We were close when we were together, but, we were separated by two thousand miles. When I was a pre-teen (tween?) we didn't have Facebook or Snapchat or text or whatever. The world was analog.

Regardless, my immediate family and I were on an island out in California. As such, we were close. My mom used to preach to us kids all the time about the importance of family. Of each other. We were the 'Fab Four'. Us against the world. This kind of thinking had an impact on me early on. I gauged others based on how they treated me and my family. Seems logical, right?

When I started acting, my mom and I became the Dynamic Duo. As I've written before, my mom was essentially my manager, chauffeur, care-taker, shoo-er (that's one who shoos) and of course, mom. My dad worked and my brother, three years my senior, still had school. When I auditioned, it was me and mom. Jobs? Me and mom. There were exceptions, of course. My brother was also auditioning for acting jobs for a while. For the most part, however, it was just the two of us. Me and my mom.

Still, the family bond was tight, and when you do something as crazy as acting in Hollywood, a tight family bond is important. Even though I was just a kid, I was still my mom's partner-in-crime, so to speak. If she was manager, chauffeur, et al...I was navigator, chief parking spotter, address finder, and passenger seat entertainer. Not that I entertained the passenger seat, but that's where

I sat while doing my entertaining. Driving in traffic, in Los Angeles of all places, is enough to quickly lose one's sanity. I was there to prevent that.

We were a team. I, of the tender age of ten, was unknowingly dependent on that team. We all are unknowingly dependent at ten, aren't we? I think we understand that we need our family, our parents, for food, safety, etc. Some people are robbed of that, I understand. But I think, in general terms, ten-year-olds understand they are dependent on the physical needs, but unknowingly dependent on the psychological needs. The love, compassion, discipline? We need this stuff, but aren't yet aware we need it. That was me, anyway.

Actors are historically insecure, self-conscious and neurotic. A generalization, of course, but we've all read the stories in People. I think it perfectly describes...People. Not the magazine, the species. I don't know of one person who at one time or another hasn't fit that bill to a T. Even the most secure, cocky, headstrong person I know. Mainly, me.

All this is to say I'm insecure, self-conscious and neurotic. At least, ten year old me. I was totally dependent on the love, maternal warmth and strength of my mom. So when I got the job of playing an eight year old little boy on television, one of two boys to a newly divorced housewife, well, what was I to think about this new "mom" in my life?

There is a moment, as a child, when you feel fear. The bogeyman in the dark, bump in the night, someone stole my woobie kind of fear. Dads are great, but kids want their mom. It's not because dad can't kick the bogeyman's butt or hold us tight and make us feel better, it's because mom's have the look. They are strong and smart and can kick the bogeyman's butt, too. But it's the look.

If Kate Jackson had only ever looked at me, she still would have been awarded the job of mom. Lucky her.

My first audition with Kate, I think I was numb, honestly. It wasn't star struck, per se, it was more, a realization of a dream. Literally. Besides, we were in a room with few people, and I was trying to get a job. I may be a clueless rube at times, but I'm not that clueless. Dumb, but not stupid. I understood why I was in that audition. The set was another matter.

In truth, I was tunnel visioned on set in the beginning. You can read that as in over my head or, at the very least, overwhelmed. Outclassed, really. I was cute, adorable even. I should have been a model. Just...Look at me. Don't ask me to say anything. I definitely should not have been a walking, talking stiff on television. I may have killed it in my audition with Kate, but I was dying on set. All of the people, the bright lights, the moving parts, the lines. Do I know my lines? What the hell had I gotten myself into??? I'm insecure, self-conscious and neurotic, I shouldn't be around people!!!

Call sheets, wardrobe, make-up, lighting, blocking, marks, action!!! *AHHHHH....*

Ever stand outside when it's cloudy and raining, and then all of a sudden it stops, and the clouds break, and you can see bright blue sky and even a little sunlight hits your face and for a brief moment the warmth envelopes you and it's a perfect day? That was Kate. The Look.

Like a true mother, she kissed my forehead, gave me a hug, asked me if I was ok, helped me find my marks, looked at me as if...As if...

As if I'd be ok. And I was. No Laurence Olivier, mind you, but I did alright. I hit my marks, said my lines, did my best to stay out of everyone's way, which is tough to do when you're four feet tall and under foot. But I managed. I managed because I had become dependent on The Look.

You can see that look on screen. You think it's different when the cameras aren't rolling, but it isn't. Kate is a great actor, but in that split second on screen, she is looking at a scared, ten year old playing an eight year old boy and with her eyes she's saying "Do you know your lines, little man?"

Actually, she's saying to me "I'm your mother!" Seriously, that's what it feels like, in that moment. For countless fans, she is believable as a mom with two kids, who loves them but leaves them with grandma so that she can go fight with Russians. Naturally. That look, though. The look is special. It's reassuring. It's acting?

One would begin to wonder how much of a rube I really am, right? I mean, she was playing a part. Was I just a gullible, needy little boy who jumped from mommy to mommy because I couldn't handle being alone for one minute?! Did I have issues? Do I still have issues? Someone, quick...Hold me!

My outburst is done. I promise. For now.

How Tall Are You?

It was acting. But it was also so much more. She cared, not only for me in that moment, but for the work. She cared for the people. It wasn't just me, but I was in the enviable position of being her youngest son. I was also the cutest human in the vicinity, so who wouldn't want to tousle my hair and love me as their son?

Ok, probably not Paul. That would be...Weird.

But Kate did. Tousle my hair, and love me as her son. I have no doubt she saw fear in my eyes that first day in the kitchen. And adult me says, yeah, it was self-preserving for her to look out for the runt who couldn't act. They had hired me after all. I was the only person to play Jamie King. They couldn't find another ten-year-old to play an eight year old. Certainly not one that was four feet tall and with hair like a motorcycle helmet. So, they were stuck with me. And Kate? Well, Kate just looked out for me. Like a mother would.

All joking aside, I did alright on set. The fear was real, but I was capable of doing the job. That's why I was there. Still, your mom tells you that you have talent and that you're good, one expects that. Your agent says it, you could make the argument they are just seeing dollar signs. My agent wasn't like that, but one could make that argument.

A casting agent thinks you have some chops, now you're getting somewhere. When Kate Jackson does it...Boom. Bonafide.

My mom tells a story of being on set one day, and we had a scene where Kate was off camera while the boys were on camera. We ran through a quick rehearsal, the crew did their thing, it was time to film. Action! Paul and I ran through the scene. His lines. My lines. All the while my mom was standing near Kate. After the director called the end of the scene, Kate looked over at my mom and whispered "He's so good."

From my perspective, Kate was family. We would celebrate Christmas in her trailer, opening gifts, eating desserts, laughing and having a great time. All of us. Paul and his family, me and my family. She would greet my mom with a hug. When my maternal grandmother came out to California from the tiny town of Galesburg, Illinois, Kate doted on her. She loved my grandma. It was special for grandma, too, because here she was, a quiet, fairly strict, certainly proper Midwestern woman, and a huge star was excited to see her. Grandma Heller never forgot that.

How Tall Are You?

When the show ended, I didn't know why. It was just, cancelled. Nobody owed me an explanation, and frankly, I never got one. It's a business, I understand. During that last year, I'm sure people were talking, but not to me. I had no idea what was going on. In truth, I was dealing with my issues at school, with other kids, with myself. I was wrapped up in my own little world. I didn't learn until much later that Kate had been sick. By then, I didn't have the slightest clue how to reach out to her.

I've heard a lot of things over the years about Kate Jackson. I've seen some headlines, but never read the articles. That really isn't my thing. Every once in a great while I'll get caught up in some Hollywood gossip, but for the most part I avoid it. I think part of it has to do with that I'm not too often star-struck. Celebrities are people, just like you and me. They do a job that is high profile and often that speaks to where we are in our own lives. It's not that we connect to *them*, we connect to their stories. Because those stories have meaning, we tend to raise the face of those stories up on a pedestal.

Sadly, our nature is also to tear that pedestal down. The theater of celebrity itself. People get engaged in the ups and downs of what happens to celebrities because it often mirrors our own ups and downs. Our own struggles.

Sometimes a celebrity makes themselves the villain, and the crowd roars when the villain stumbles. Other times we see the self-destruction, and we shake our heads in disgust, only to root for the comeback. It most certainly is theater.

We forget one crucial element to this type of theater, however. Celebrities are people. Real people. Real feelings, real problems, real struggles. Everyone has their own insecurities. With our insecurities or our own struggles, the last thing we'd want is for someone to make light of them. And yet, that is what we do to others, as if their job of entertaining us on screen or stage somehow also means they have to suffer our entertainment of their lives as well. I'm not buying it. Or buying into it.

Besides, I rarely believe the sensational headlines I see anyway. It's clickbait, designed to pull you into the muck and get your hands dirty. Do I really want to rely on the unnamed source of "someone close to the situation" for information that a celebrity is actually a robot with a special U.S. military battery that will keep them alive? FOREVER? No. I do not want to rely on that unnamed source. Nor do I care of such celeb-bot.

Maybe it's naïveté. Ignorance, maybe. Anyway, that's my rant.

You want to know who Kate Jackson is? Read all the crap online you want. And then read this. Scarecrow and Mrs. King used to film for so many months out of the year, I don't recall exactly how many, but for argument's sake, let's say nine. Those are long months for the principal actors. Long days, long nights. Sometimes six, seven days a week, collaborating on a project together with multiple moving parts. These shows are always filmed with deadlines looming overhead. I won't say filming a T.V. show has the urgency of brain surgery, but don't let anyone tell you it isn't hard work. It is.

The cast and crew put in their time. Closely knit, together. For nine months straight. And then a show goes on hiatus. That's the break between this season and next season, if there is a next season. Some shows, like Firefly, are still on hiatus. Not that I'm bitter. Anyway, the hiatus period was when actors and crew would seek other jobs, to continue working throughout the year. Often, people would take vacations to rest and recharge from such a brutal filming schedule during the season.

For me, hiatus meant going back to school to finish up my school year, and then summer break, which meant sleeping in, swimming, fighting with my brother and lots and lots of daydreaming about space. Or mountains. Or buried treasure. You get the idea. Kids stuff. I wasn't worried about work. I did, though. I worked. I continued to audition for commercials, and was hired for a few. My hiatus was about me. Being lost in my own little world, a common theme in this book, you'll notice.

Kate Jackson was on hiatus too. I couldn't tell you what she did, because again, I was in my own little world. She knew that, though, because during our hiatus from the show, Kate would call my house and check in with my mom...To see how I was doing. To see how we all were doing. They would chat for a while, my mom would fill her in, and then that was it until the next call. I was clueless. I didn't find out until years later, as an adult.

The rumors, the tabloids, the whatever...Read it, don't read it. There isn't a perfect person out there, and none of us wouldn't want to live our lives in a bubble. You want to know who Kate Jackson was, and I'm sure still is? This. Kate Jackson is a woman who took the time to check on people she cared about. Without fanfare or seeking adulation, recognition or validation. Just, picking up the phone and having a conversation.

I'll leave you with this. For me, Kate Jackson is family.

OKLAHOMA

2 MAY 1985

Dear greg,

...Your a great actor. Keep up the great work.

19 DEC 1985

Dear greg,

...Please do not innore my letter I want a photo 4 real.
Please treat your fans nice.

Mike K.
Enid, OK

Before I make light of Mike's two letters, let me first
say, in all sincerity, I hope he got an autographed photo.
Honest. It may seem like I got a ton of fan mail, but really
I didn't. I wasn't a huge star, and Mike is right, it's
important to treat my fans nice.

Mike's first letter must have taken a page out of the
Nebraska girl's book, literally, as the note was a torn piece

of paper. I guess because he only wrote so much, he felt like he could use the top 3/4 for something else. Maybe a letter to Paul?

The second letter was actually a card wishing me Happy Holidays, written in a blank notecard with a reproduced painting of a duck and frog in a pond on the front. Mike asked about my favorite sports, hobbies, if I had a big family or any pets at home.

Though this may be a little repetitive, let me address those questions.

My favorite sport is baseball. But back then it was probably skateboarding. No, probably swimming. During the time I was on Scarecrow and Mrs. King we lived in a house in Claremont with a pool. I loved that pool. It was quite difficult for my mom to get me out of that pool.

I don't know that I had a hobby, although now that I type that I think my hat collection qualifies. I had a hat collection. I had too many hats to remember. My dad was a transportation executive, and traveled a lot. Every time he visited a new building, he'd come home with a hat and give it to me. I never wore them, but tucked them away inside my closet. If we went to Disneyland, I bought a hat.

Germany? A Tyrolean hat. Tijuana, Mexico? I bought a leather cowboy hat. My obsession grew and continued until I was married, when I realized I had boxes (plural) in the garage of hats I'd never remembered even seeing before. That's when the hobby ended.

I have a small family. My brother and I are both 5' 5" and my mom is 5' 2" (but she thinks she's taller). Wait..What? Oh...Quantity not physical size? Got it. Yep, still small.

I grew up with a short legged mutt named Sugar. Only a manly name for our pet, I say. I loved that dog. Just imagine if Chewbacca was about ankle high and had four legs, that was Sugar.

CAR WARS

People don't realize what a big star Bruce Boxleitner is. And by that, I mean, he's tall. Freakishly tall. Six feet, two inches, if the internet is any authority, and why would the internet lie? He could, in fact, write a book titled "How Tall Are You?", and it be appropriate. But late. I'm writing that book first.

Ok, maybe not freakishly tall. One of my best friends is 6' 3", and one of his best friends is 6' 6". That's freakishly tall. Not Shaq tall, but then again, who is? I categorize anyone not five feet, five inches to be freakishly tall, mind you. Enough about that.

The first thing most people notice about Bruce is that he's pretty. Handsome, I mean. Pretty handsome. I don't see it. I mean, he's too tall and generally, I can't see up that far to see how pretty handsome he is. Ok, maybe one more height joke for good measure.

He *is* a good looking guy. Classic Hollywood. Tall, full head of hair, great smile. It really is no wonder he has been a Hollywood leading man for so long. Be in close proximity to Bruce for any length of time and guaranteed at least one woman will mention how good looking he is. It happens every time. It's gotta be tough on the guy, you know?

This fact, by the way, is something I learned early on in my time on Scarecrow and Mrs. King. Like, day one. My mom, you see, thinks Bruce is handsome. She wasn't shy about saying so, either. To me. To my dad. To Bruce, I'm sure. She would not have been the first, nor will she be the last. Bruce is a good looking guy. But enough about that.

I was actually a fan of Bruce's before we met. *How the West Was Won?* Nope. *East of Eden?* Nope. *Kenny Rogers' The Gambler?* Nope. *Tron?!??* Uh...Nope. Bruce as adventurer and big game trapper Frank Buck in all seventeen episodes of *Bring'Em Back Alive!* Beginning in 1981, young me could be found lost in the worlds of Choose Your Own Adventure books, a little known Steven Spielberg film called Raiders of the Lost Ark, a no-jokes-about-it little known T.V. show called Tales of the Gold Monkey, and in the winter of 1982/1983, the very short run, previously mentioned Bring'Em Back Alive!

I must have had a thing for khaki.

Actually, I have a thing for high adventure. Nobody can dispute that Raiders of the Lost Ark, the inspiration for the television adventure shows to follow, was the most polished and well done piece of those I mentioned. Let's face it, that movie is arguably one of the best ever made. But that's a discussion for another time. If I'm being honest, of the T.V. shows, I preferred Tales of the Gold Monkey, if only for the Grumman Goose amphibious plane.

Bruce's show was different, though, in that it harkened back to a completely different world, that of the trapper. It had more of a Rudyard Kipling feel to it, than say, Indiana Jones. It's a niche, for sure, but a commendable niche to chase. Who doesn't love a dashing young man in a pith helmet? That's the thing about movies and television, you never know what is going to catch on with audiences. Sure, there are the usual medical or police procedurals, but television audiences are also looking for something...Different. Like maybe, a spy who recruits a housewife to help him fight Russians.

As I had mentioned, Bruce is good looking. It's kind of a running joke, because while many may be focused on his looks, he is a great actor. Old school, and, to be honest, I hate that term. There really isn't another way to describe Bruce, though. He is professional, manly, has a great sense of humor. He's a true cowboy, really. For a ten year old kid, though, you don't get any of that.

When I think back of my first meeting with Bruce, I can't help but focus on how much of a presence he was. I don't want to beat it into the ground, but he was the center of attention because all of the ladies thought he was so gorgeous. And he was. He is. But get inside that circle that hovers around him, and he's funny and approachable. To a kid, he was this guy everyone looked up to and he made time to chat and be playful.

That was really all we had, because early on we didn't work together. If we were in the same scene, it's because Lee was in the bushes trying to get Amanda's attention. Bruce would be on set, joking about being in the bushes, talking with all of the guys, all of the women. Really just friendly with everyone. But a professional actor. Bruce likes to have fun, but when the cameras roll, he's all business.

I've said it before, that was basically my experience with all of the actors on the show. They were all professionals. Except for me, of course. I was just trying to see over the counter in the kitchen and not trip on the rug in the living room.   Ok, so maybe I was a true professional.

That circle around Bruce forms as much for his stories as it does for his looks. More so, actually. I wasn't kidding when I wrote Bruce was a true cowboy. He was. He is. Look at his film credits from the late Seventies and early Eighties and it's mostly westerns. And when you see all of the stars' names that appear alongside Bruce's, what you're seeing is the headline of a story, because Bruce has a million of them.

I have a confession. Actually, I have two confessions. First, and we'll get back to this in a minute, I'm a sucker for a good story. It's one of the reasons I love to write. I'm always trying my best to tell a good story. Second, I may have slightly mischievous reasons for talking about how pretty Bruce is. I told him I was writing this book, and he asked me to be nice. Ha ha ha...Ahem.

Giving the man a razzing about his Hollywood good looks is about as low as I can go. Honestly, I don't have any dirt on the man, and even if I did, I probably wouldn't write about it. He's a friend, and though others may spill dirt to sell books, I'm sorry to disappoint you. Anyway,

Bruce Boxleitner just isn't interesting enough for a full Tell-All-Book. There isn't anything to tell. Is he perfect? No. And neither am I. Or you. Or that guy in the seat across from you trying to read the cover of this book wondering why you look so disappointed right now. *What book would do that to a human being??*

I love Bruce. He makes me laugh. He can be grumpy, which makes me laugh even more. He has an opinion on just about everything, which I relate to, but I don't agree with everything he has to say, and that's okay. I think that makes us human, right? He has great stories, and it's fun to sit and hang out with him and just...Listen. He has a story for everything or everyone. He is a great storyteller, weaving his tales with wonderful enthusiasm. Even if he's told the story before (which he has) or you even heard the story before (which you might have). If you just sit and listen, it's always entertaining.

Of course, my fondest memories have come in the years since Scarecrow and Mrs. King. I've met up with Bruce a number of times for fan events. Even though years have passed since we've seen each other, you'd never know it. Each time it's like picking up right where we left off.

"There is my t.v. son!" He says in his booming voice.

How Tall Are You?

You'll find he is either coming or going. He has a natural way of making these entrances, and because he is a tall man, his comings and goings are a thing. He enters a room and people know he's there. Often because he's laughing and talking with someone. Anyone. Bruce loves to laugh and he loves to talk. He has so many stories.

I lied. I have one disparaging thing to say about Bruce. It's more of a personal preference thing, so my guess is you'll disagree. I get it, you love him. He's tall. He's handsome. But he ain't perfect, people. He hated the Porsche.

So I have to draw the line about how great Bruce Boxleitner is. I mean, come on! He hated the Porsche? I'm (mostly) kidding, but really? Ok, the car was notorious for breaking down, which makes it difficult when you're all prepared to do a scene but your beautiful, topless, twenty year old German co-star isn't. But it was a Porsche. A 356 Cabriolet. That car was a masterpiece of art on wheels.

I've been in love with Porsches since, since, since...Since I took a little trip to Germany when I was, like, eleven years old? A long time. The hero in my novels drives Porsches! (Shameless Plug) It's a freakin' Porsche!!

And what, Bruce Boxleitner is too good for that car? Why...Because he's tall, and that car wasn't great for tall people? So now we have to boo-hoo this man because he's tall? And good looking?! I won't do it! I can't!

In truth, it made more sense for a six foot two, American spy to drive good ole American muscle anyway. The 1984 Chevrolet Corvette C4. It was bigger, faster, and undeniably more technologically superior to the Porsche 356. And it ran, which, if you ask Bruce, was a real selling point. As I said, it made more sense. But who wants to make sense? If they had put Bruce into a 1963 Corvette C2? Then, I would have been altogether a happy man. Genuinely an iconic car. Some would argue the same of the C4, sure. It was Eighties, I'll give'm that.

I love old things. Old houses. Old cars. Yeah, I like old people. Not so much old food, but you get the point. History. Vintage. Clothes, that kind of stuff. Things that tell a story. Like Bruce. He's getting old. I love the guy.

For me, it's nice to have adult conversations with people I knew as a child. The relationship has changed. I get to hear stories I wasn't privy to as a child. I can hear a perspective on things completely different than my own from four feet off the ground. I enjoy seeing Bruce because he's family. Like that fatherly uncle you only see every few years because he's off trapping big game, catching Russian spies or flying off into space on some grand adventure. Lucky for us, he has a story to tell.

PENNSYLVANIA

Dear Greg,

Me and my friend think you are adorable.

...My name is Lori and hers is Allison. Who are the cutest girls around. Everybody likes us but we pick you.

...Also I would like to include that we watch Scarecrow and Mrs. King all the time to see you. But I like it.

Lori A.

Hazelton, PA

Dear Sirs,

Would you kindly send me photo's of Greg Morton and Paul Stout?

Naomi C.

Honesdale, PA

Dear Scarecrow and Mrs. King,

...I think your show is great and I love every one minute of it.

...I am writing about Paul Stout and Greg Mort. I think there just good looking.

...I think they should get more lines.

Sandy C.
Norristown, PA

Dear Greg,

...I collect unicorns, rabbits, anything that is purple and pictures from stars. I would like to know some things about you. How did you get started in acting? When did you start acting? Do you enjoy acting? When is your birthday? What is your favorite color. Do you have a fan club, I would like to join.

Diane D.
Indiana, PA

Dear Greg,

3-10-86   11:20pm

I'm one of your biggest fans.

...How long have you been on the show? Where you ever on any other shows besides Scarecrow and Mrs. King?

How Tall Are You?

...How long have you been acting?

...Are you friends with anyone on the show in real life?

Donna D.

Indiana, PA

Dear Greg,

Will you go with me?

Amy G.

Morrisdale, PA

Dear Greg,

I think you are very cute.

...I am 10 1/2 years old. I don't have glasses in my shool picture I sent you, but I have glasses now.

Erin K.

Warren, PA

Dear Greg,

Hi how are you. fine I hope. I'm fine.

...Will you do other shows?

Ruth M.

Bolivar, PA

How Tall Are You?

Dear Greg,

...You are quite a handsome man and you seem to have a great personality.

...I would like to know if I may please have a photograph of yourself.

...I hope you don't disappoint me.

> *Joan R.*
> *Bethlehem, PA*

Dear Greg Morton,

...Do you go to school?

...I really like watching Scarecrow and Mrs. King and I would really like to talk to you sometime.

> *Amy W.*
> *Chambersburg, PA*

How Tall Are You?

Dear Greg,

...I think you are a real hunk. I have about 5 pictures hanging up in my room. Greg how hold are you. Will you go with me.

P.S. I play basketball and softball

Jodi Y.
Vintondale, PA

Lori and Allison are the cutest girls around, but they picked me. I think for dodgeball. I was pretty good at dodgeball growing up, and if I was going to get picked for something, it would have been that. It certainly wouldn't have been for football. Or anything with a height requirement.

There was no envelope for Naomi's letter, which probably accounts for why I got a letter addressed to "Dear Sirs". I have never been so plural.

Like Sandy C., I think we should have gotten more lines. Beginning with the rest of the letters of my name.

Diane D. and Donna D. were sisters, though they never mentioned each other. I surmised the relationship based on the return address label in Indiana, PA. How confusing to live in such a town. People ask, "Where do you live?" "Indiana". "Where in Indiana?" "Pennsylvania".

My favorite color is blue. I was with the show from the beginning, having appeared in the very first episode of Scarecrow and Mrs. King. I recommend reading this book for the rest of the answers to your questions, but no, I don't have a fan club. I think I'd have to be a real celebrity for that sort of thing.

Amy and Jodi both wanted to go with me. I'm flattered. Jodi, in fact, was quite smitten, including real lipstick kisses on her letter. Jodi had 5 pictures on her wall, but never clarified they were of me, which I'm guessing they weren't. It was probably Corey Haim. Anyway, Jodi's mentioning of basketball was a dig at my height, I think.

Erin K. also thought I was cute, but she needed glasses. Enough said. I don't blame her for making that distinction. Plausible deniability and all.

To answer Ruth's question...Yes. I will do other shows. But so far, nobody has asked. Other than that I'm fine. We're all fine here.

Joan, on the other hand, thought I was quite the handsome man. Her letter was postmarked October of 1983. I was ten. In her defense, I'm probably the same height I was back then. I'm not sure if that is a real defense or not, but that's what I'm going with.

I did go to school, Amy. On set and back at home. I wasn't terribly good at it, until I got to college. Looking back, I wish I had focused more on school. I encourage everyone to get an education. I think it's important.

I didn't do the math, but it seems that Pennsylvania was the home to most of my fan mail. All from females. I've never been, but if they really love me this much, I've been missing out.

A CLASS ACT

If Kate Jackson is an Angel, Beverly Garland was God herself, as holy analogies go. And I loved her...Oh how I loved her. One can't not love Beverly Garland, in my opinion. She was everything you want your grandmother to be; smart, funny, no nonsense. She commanded respect the minute she walked on set, not because she announced it or she demanded it or she even talked about respect. She commanded it because of the way she carried herself. She was a lady, she was a professional. She was a class act.

I considered titling this chapter "Gunslinger", after one of Beverly's early western credits. Yeah, she was a western star. Before Bruce. Look back at any of the pictures from that time and you'll see a young, beautiful, gun toting Beverly. The complete package. For me, gunslinger describes her wit best. She was sharp, and not afraid to speak her mind. But never disrespectful. She earned respect because she gave it. She just never took any grief from anyone. Professional.

I was a clown on set. An entertainer. The monkey dancing in the street for a nickel. Kate was the drive, the ambition. Kate was invested in every aspect of what was happening on set, from the script, to the camera to the lights. I'm sure she felt enormous responsibility for all the people employed by the show, and, well, Kate is a perfectionist. It shows in her energy. Beverly? I have no doubt Beverly felt the same pressures every actor does for the success of the show. You'd just never know it. She was a rock.

I'm a huge baseball fan. Each year I watch the World Series. It's especially satisfying when the Cubs win, like they did in 2016. I won't even pretend that wasn't a shameless shout out to my Cubs. Anyway, each year I watch the Series, and each year there is a tense moment in a game for one or both teams, and the cameras turn toward the dugout, and while I'm wringing my hands sitting on my couch, the managers are all stone faced like they're standing in their kitchen waiting for their coffee to finish brewing.

That was Beverly Garland.

In between takes, while the crew busily hummed around her, Beverly Garland would sit in her studio chair and knit. She knew her lines, knew her cues, knew well enough to let the camera techs and lighting techs and sounds techs and set techs all do their job. She had the experience that came with a distinguished career, and as is often the case on a set, knew that waiting was a big part of the game for actors.

Waiting is an oft overlooked aspect of what film and television actors do. One would think, how difficult is it to wait? It isn't difficult in the sense that anyone standing around doing nothing is essentially 'waiting'. You can wait sitting down, wait standing, wait lying on a couch or the floor behind the craft services table, though I wouldn't recommend that last one. The craft services table is popular, not very quiet (unless cameras are rolling) and a good place to have juice or a condiment spilled on you by an eleven year old boy.

The waiting isn't difficult in and of itself, but acting is a profession of movement. Action and reaction. Physical movement, emotional movement. Film and television is a visual medium, a moving, visual medium. And thus, waiting, or more accurately, the absence of any meaningful movement, is the antithesis of what actors need. Models are better at waiting than most actors.

You're probably still thinking, actors can't wait...Why? It kills energy. It saps them of the movement they need to deliver the performance you want. What's that saying? A body in motion stays in motion? Actors need the energy of movement. Good actors, though, have learned to shut down between takes while the crew is staging the next shot, and then ramp up and re-engage the energy they need for the performance. Good actors will outwardly move, talk, sing, yell, jump up and down like they're in boot camp, all to re-engage that energy.

Great actors will put their knitting down, walk twenty feet to their mark, wait for their cue, deliver their line and make it all seem as easy as opening the refrigerator for milk. Great actors like Beverly Garland. Seriously, the woman gave the whole craft of acting an illusion of simplicity, when it is anything but.

If you ever get a chance to watch a great actor work, you'll know they're great by the ease with which they make things appear. It's the same in sports. Hall of Fame baseball player Ken Griffey Jr. was accused of being lazy or not trying hard enough during his days playing for the Seattle Mariners and Cincinnati Reds. Of course, those accusing him didn't understand the nuance of greatness, that great players make the game look easy. I run out in the field chasing a fly ball like I'm escaping a pride of charging lions because I'm not a great baseball player. Junior trotted to a sharply hit ball like he was chasing butterflies because the man knew he'd catch it. And he did.

Beverly Garland is a Hall of Famer.

Of all the people I've worked with, Beverly is the one I miss the most. She is my constant reminder to seize the day, take opportunities as they come to you, and don't listen to the doubts that creep into your mind that sound like other people's voices. I'll explain.

I haven't always been keen on being recognized as a part of Scarecrow and Mrs. King. It's not because I'm not proud to have been a part of the show, but because I had walked away from show business. I didn't realize that I could appreciate my career and celebrate it without being a working actor. It probably won't come as a surprise, but when Scarecrow and Mrs. King ended, so did my career in show business.

I continued to audition for a while, but never got hired and, we'll discuss it in depth later, I was in a bad place emotionally. Nevertheless, I finished school, entered the workforce and became a contributing member of society.

How Tall Are You?

I never discussed my work as a child actor. By early adulthood, my physical features had changed and I was far enough removed from the show that nobody recognized me. I was okay with that, because as I've written before, I was unknowingly in search of a balanced life.

I've always kept one foot in the door of creativity. Since my early teens I've written poetry, sketched, drawn, thought and dreamt. I'm full of ideas, many of which are unrealized. Unfinished. Fragments. I have notebooks and notebooks of my mind on paper. It is how my mind works. I don't know that I'm attention deficit, but.

What was I saying? I'm kidding, of course. My point was that I've always been creative, even if I walked away from the one creative outlet I'd known my entire life. Performing. A large part of it was due to being bullied in school. That led me away from being completely extroverted into being mostly introverted. In many ways, it began a period of increased anxiety about standing in front of people and entertaining. Public speaking is most people's number one fear. It wasn't for me. I'd been standing in front of people like a dancing monkey forever.

But I was done.

How does this relate to Beverly? She hosted the 25th Anniversary of Scarecrow and Mrs. King at her hotel. Bruce was there. Martha was there. Beverly was there. Paul Stout was there. Kate wasn't, but I think she'd been dealing with some personal issues and public anxiety of her own. And for her, it's ten-fold because she's Kate. The press are all over big stars for a scoop, real or, in most cases, imagined. Rag magazines aren't taking pictures of me when I walk out of my house. My face won't sell the Daily News.

I was invited to the Anniversary, it's just...I didn't go. I passed. It wasn't all that long ago, but I was still in a place in my life where I wasn't sure I could balance celebrating that world without being a part of it. I was still struggling with identity. For many people, I think we struggle with identity our whole lives.

The event was held on October 3rd and 4th of 2008. Beverly died two months later, on December 5th. I hadn't seen the woman in over twenty years. She had been my grandmother for four years. She was family, and I missed an opportunity to wrap my arms around her and tell her I loved her. Tell her what she meant to me. This big star. She treated me with kindness and love and even a little gruff, which was to be expected because, well, I can be a pain in the ass.

It's difficult not being able to say thank you to those who've meant something to you. It's even more difficult when you realize you had the chance and you made a decision not to take advantage of an opportunity. It stings. Beverly is the one I'll miss the most.

She was a fire-cracker, let me tell you. And when she cared about you, all others better be on high alert, because Beverly would look out for you. She walked with her head high, full of confidence. I just don't know how anyone couldn't love this woman.

Case in point, the Warner Bros. studio party in 1984.

Imagine a soundstage full of Hollywood's elite, all gathered for a private celebration. The room decorated for a party. People, everywhere. It was like a prom for anyone associated with Warner Bros. But with wine.

"Oh, I loved you in that thing!"
"My DAHHHH-LING!"
"Call my people."

How Tall Are You?

Yeah, so. All these people, and me. As my mom tells the story, Burt Reynolds was there. Clint Eastwood, too. Mark Singer, remember him? I remember being happy about that because we were huge fans of the show "V". Honestly, not that I remember that any of these people were there. I don't get that star struck. I never really have. There are few exceptions of course. And apparently, former NFL great, the late Lyle Alzado, was one exception.

My family and I sat at the Scarecrow and Mrs. King table, for lack of a better title. It was me, my mom, dad and brother, and Beverly Garland. I'm sure others were there, but hey, memories. As my mom tells the story, all I could talk about was Lyle Alzado. This hulking, beast of a man was at the party, no doubt surrounded by celebrities who thought he was the coolest thing. And apparently, I thought he was the coolest thing, because I couldn't stop talking about him. But I wouldn't approach him.

A little back story. I had a broken arm at the time. I had been at the World Famous Upland Pipeline Skate Park and dropped into a pool, but my skateboard had flipped out from under me, and as I fell I reached my arm back to catch myself. CRACK! I broke both my ulna and humerus bones about two inches above my wrist. Clean breaks. I knew it the moment it happened. So at the time of the party, I was sporting a cast on my right arm. A cast I wouldn't let anyone sign or touch with a marker.

FUN FACT: You can see my cast in the Scarecrow and Mrs. King Season 3 episode The Triumvirate when I leave the kitchen at the end of the episode.

What does any of this have to do with Beverly Garland? I'm getting to that.

I wanted Lyle Alzado's autograph, but I was just too shy to approach him and ask. Maybe he just had too many people around him. Maybe because he was 6' 3" and I was closer to 3' 6" (otherwise known as underfoot). Anyway, I was sitting at the table and apparently *not* shy about my desire to have the man's autograph, and Beverly wasn't having it. If I wanted that autograph, by God, she was going to make it happen! She stood up, grabbed me by the good arm, and marched me over, through the crowd of people, and introduced me to Lyle Freakin' Alzado!

Beverly: "Hi, I'm Beverly Garland, nice to meet you. This young man is Greg Morton, and he's a big fan and would love you to autograph his cast."
Me: "Duh, duh, duhduhduhduh..."

Lyle Freakin' Alzado: "Yes ma'am. I'll do anything you ask because you're kind and sweet and I'm afraid of you."

Me: "Duh, duh, duhduhduhduh..."

Or something like that. I still have that cast. I made sure the nurse was especially careful when cutting it off my arm. Knock on wood those were the only bones I've ever broken, and Lyle Alzado was the only signature that cast ever saw.

Thanks to Beverly Garland.

The moral of the story? If you get a chance to see someone you haven't seen in a long time, take it. Wrap your arms around that person and tell them what they mean to you. Beverly Garland was in my life for a short period of time, all things considered, but she had lasting impact. I am who I am today, in part because of her influence. She reaffirmed the importance of professionalism, of looking out for others, and also of having a good time. She reaffirmed what it means to be a class act.

I miss her.

SOUTH CAROLINA

19 OCT 1983

Dear Greg,

...Please send me your age and date of birth. Also please send the me the latest color or black + white picture of yourself.

Harry H.
Greenville, SC

26 JUN 1985

Dear Greg

...Please send me your age and date of birth.

...Please make it a color picture, if you can.

...Are you left handed or right handed? Please write your age and date of birth on the back of your picture.

20 OCT 1986

Dear Greg

...Please send me the <u>latest</u> color or black + white picture of yourself. Please write your date of birth...

...Please write if your are left or right handed...

Harry H.

Greenville, SC

A couple of things about letters like Harry's; First, the three letters are from the same Harry. Why did I break them up like I did? Because they came from two different addresses in Greenville. In my mind, that warrants separating them like I did. My brain, my book, my rules.

Next, in re-reading these letters after so many years, I get concerned that I didn't write these fans back when I get multiple letters from the same person. In my defense, these letters didn't get mailed directly to me. They would get mailed to CBS (either Los Angeles or New York), the studio lot in Burbank or my agent in Hollywood. There is no telling how long it then took some of these letters to reach me because, let's face it, a letter sent to Burbank Studios for Greg Morton isn't going to be a top priority for the kid in the mailroom who had absolutely no clue who I was. If they had sent them to Danny Pintauro, maybe.

What really struck me as odd was that they were all essentially the same exact letter. So much time between each letter, and the wording and phrasing is nearly identical. As demanding as Harry was about my age, he never revealed his own. Or anything else about himself for that matter.

For the record I was ten, twelve and thirteen. Also I'm right-handed, for the most part. Sometimes I bat left-handed, but it depends on who is pitching.

DEAD RINGER

I've never worked with Martha Smith.

Of course, Scarecrow and Mrs. King fans are going to tell me different. But, unfortunately, I don't remember ever working with Martha Smith, so that's it.

End of chapter.

I'm kidding, of course. About the end of chapter thing. Though I seriously don't remember ever working with Martha. I did, early in the series of course. The fourteenth episode of Season One, Dead Ringer. Martha had dual roles, as both Agency operative Francine Desmond and Hungarian defector Magda Petrak, an ungrateful shrew who invades the King home, doesn't like Amanda's coffee, and ruins Phillip's day with a soliloquy about how second place is for losers. Which, to be fair, is true. But second place are the first losers, so there's that.

How Tall Are You?

My best 'past memory' of Martha Smith is meeting her again as an adult when she and I crashed a fan event being held for Bruce Boxleitner. We'd been invited, but it wasn't a Scarecrow and Mrs. King thing. Just a Bruce thing, for Fansource. It was maybe the earliest reunion for the show, way back in 2001.

That reunion was memorable for a number of reasons. It was the first opportunity to see old friends I hadn't seen since 1987. Second, it was proof to my wife that I was actually on television with these people, and not just some sad little man making things up. Also, it was a chance to reconnect with Martha Smith.

Truth is, I don't really have any Martha stories from my childhood. We didn't really work together, so we never really got a chance to know each other. If I'm being honest, like brutally honest, I didn't have an interest in knowing who she was. Not because of anything she ever said or did, but I was a child and singularly focused on what was in front of my large round face, and because she wasn't there, she wasn't interesting to me. That was probably for the best, because I'm not sure we would have made any sort of connection.

That all sounds horrible. Let me try and explain, and hopefully not make things worse for myself.

Have you ever worked with someone in the same building, but didn't work *with* them? You've seen them, maybe in the break room or the parking lot. You've never really spoken to each other, but you both each know the other exists? You don't really have an opinion one way or the other, but nothing compels either one of you to walk over to the other and extend a greeting? And then, one day a project comes along and the two of you have to meet and suddenly you realize this person is very interesting and you enjoy spending time with them, and it hits you that you've been in proximity of a friend for a long time and never known it?

That was Martha and me.

She'll probably tell you she tolerates the runt she sits next to at autograph shows, just to be nice. It's okay. I really wouldn't blame her. I have that effect on beautiful women. Ask my wife.

I'm kidding of course. I hope. Martha has always been sweet and kind and funny with me. We enjoy spending time together. In truth, I love her. She defies all expectations when you see her from the other end of the room. The cover of the book is beautiful, blonde and always laughing or smiling. You now have a picture in your head? A stereotype, no doubt. I'm sure she has been fighting that stereotype her entire life.

This woman is smart, inquisitive and clever. She is *not* Babs Jansen. When you watch the episode Dead Ringer, you should see two things. First, Martha is super-hot as a natural blonde, but could arguably be hotter as a brunette. Sexist, I know, but let's face it, this woman is beautiful. Where was I? Oh, right, stereotypes. *Ironic, no?* Once she begins her lines, the second thing you'll notice is a real intelligence and talent that we didn't often get to see from Martha in Francine. Not because it wasn't there, but because the material wasn't there.

Martha has the chops. I would love to see her in a full on kick down, drag out drama role, I think she would kill it. I know this because, in the few years that we've gotten together for autograph shows, one of my favorite things to do is just chat Martha up. World events, her life, anything. She has a great perspective on life, and has seen quite a lot. I think she would bring a unique perspective to a dramatic role. She's been through stuff, and is one tough woman.

I was probably in my thirties before I ever saw Animal House. I just never had an interest. I'm kind of a kook that way. Popular, even iconic movies will sometimes turn my interest off. I'll watch a blockbuster, but if it gets too much hype, then I tend to shy away. Also, I'm not drawn to comedies. Luckily, Animal House exceeded all of my expectations, and Martha was fantastic. It wasn't the first college comedy movie to come along, but it certainly set the bar for everything that came after it.

Anyway, that movie, Martha's most famous role to that point, never had an influence on my perception of Martha. I always knew her as Francine whom I never worked with.

One last thing. I think we get along so well, in part, because Martha is a kook, too. At an autograph show in Los Angeles recently, we were sitting off to ourselves before a photo shoot, and just talking. I'm constantly asking her questions about everything because, well, I want to know everything about her. So we were sitting there talking, and somehow the subject of crying on cue had come up.

"I can cry on cue." Martha said to me.

"I have no doubt."

"Want to see me do it?"

"Absolutely, that would be awesome."

Martha's face got serious. Her eyes began to shine.

"Wait...Here? Now?" I blurted out, astonished.

"Gimme a second, I can do it."

Her eyes began to water.

"Wait, you can't do this now! People are going to think I'm being mean to you." I pleaded. I was really worried people were going to think I was being insulting. I would never! "Besides, we're about to get our pictures taken. You don't want red eyes for that."

She stopped, and then smiled. Like she wasn't on the verge of a breakdown a half second before. Basically, my heart had stopped. I thought she was going to cry and everyone was going to look at me like I was being a big fat jerk.

A second later she laughed. That infectious, Martha laugh.

TEXAS

Dear "Scarecrow and Mrs. King",
I've already gotten an autographed picture, and now
I'd love to get sheet music for your title song...

Marc M.
El Paso, TX

Second largest state in the Union and I got one letter. Asking for sheet music.

KIDDS for KIDS in AFRICA

In 1984, Boomtown Rats lead singer Bob Geldof wrote "Do They Know It's Christmas?" a song performed by the U.K. supergroup Band Aid. It was written and released as a charity album to raise money and awareness of the famine that was devastating Ethiopia. The song was a huge international hit, and has been a radio staple at Christmastime ever since.

The success of the U.K. single inspired American greats Harry Belafonte, Quincy Jones, Lionel Ritchie and none other than Michael Jackson to produce a song of their own, "We Are the World". The song was released on March 8th, 1985, and quickly rose to No. 1 on the charts. Seriously, if I'm telling you something you don't already know you are either too young to remember or you never turned on the radio in 1985. For those of you that are too young, look it up. It was a historic accomplishment in the world of music that has never been duplicated.

How Tall Are You?

In 1984 and 1985, NBC aired a live action/cartoon show on Saturdays called Kidd Video. It was a musical thing, intended to help capture a young MTV audience. Can you tell I've researched this stuff? Anyway, it was a popular show, and musically oriented, so naturally, if all of these adults were doing their part to raise money and awareness, why couldn't kids do the same?

On the heels of the success of "We Are the World", Kidd Video produced "Kidds for Kids in Africa"; a video featuring the song "Love's Going to Find a Way". And because it was Kidd Video, they invited nearly 70 child actors to participate as back-up singers for the song. Enter a four foot tall wonder-munchkin with an exceptionally large head. That'd be me, in case you were wondering.

They must have been hard up for *stars*. Just call me filler.

All the truly big names in Hollywood Child-dom were there. Todd Bridges, Jason Bateman, Joey Lawrence, Kim Fields, Malcolm-Jamal Warner, that dude from Karate Kid that picks on Daniel. All the big names. Also, Sean Astin, just shy of a month after the release of his breakout hit The Goonies. With Sean was his little brother Mackenzie, who was making a name for himself alongside Kim Fields on

The Facts of Life. I got placed next to Mackenzie, probably because he was one of the few people there that didn't tower over me.

As far as the singing went, the job was easy. Stand in one spot. Smile a lot. Join in the chorus, which meant sing the words "Love's gonna find a waaaayyy..." about a million times. Smile a lot.

Cut.

Wrap!

Good stuff. News outlets were there to help promote the event. I was on the news. Not talking, mind you. Nobody wants to hear me talk. Just looking into the camera. And smiling. I'm good at that. It was a cool day, getting to meet and hang out with a bunch of colleagues. They were all people I'd recognized from television or had seen in auditions. It was one of the most memorable days of being a "celebrity".

Mackenzie, his brother Sean, and their father, John Astin, were really what made the day for me, though. Don't get me wrong, I'm honored to have been a part of something that has incredible meaning, and I hope had a positive impact on lives in Africa. The thing is, once my part in the music video was over, I didn't have anything relating to that impact of Africa to hold on to. I wasn't part of Kidd Video, and so I didn't participate in any further promotion or get word on how successful our work was in helping other kids. I'm left with the experience I had of that single day, and nothing was more of an experience than lunch with the Astins.

Mackenzie and Sean are the sons of Patty Duke, in case you didn't know. Patty Duke was the star of, well, many things, but for me most notably "The Patty Duke Show", in which she played cousins...Identical cousins, all the way. One pair of matching bookends, different as night and day. As a kid, I enjoyed re-runs of the show.

Mackenzie and Sean are also the sons of Patty's then husband, John Astin (hence the surname), in case you didn't know. John Astin was the star of, well, many things, but for me most notably "The Addams Family", in which he played the patriarch Gomez Addams. Creepy and kooky. Mysterious and spooky. Altogether ooky. Yep...As a kid, I enjoyed re-runs of the show.

Sensing a theme here? I watched a lot of t.v., yes. As a kid, I watched a lot of black and white television, not because I'm so old we didn't have color t.v., but because the best shows were all the older shows. The intelligence of the older sitcoms generally beats out anything they produce today, in my opinion. I may be biased. I watched these shows in part because I was too young to stay up for a lot of the primetime television and these sitcoms were played during the day on the weekends. So when I got a chance to meet Mackenzie and Sean, and then was invited to have lunch together with their dad, it was an opportunity I wasn't about to pass up.

Mackenzie and I hit it off immediately. Standing next to each other for the better part of the day, it was nice to have someone who shared similar interests, had a similar sense of humor and was someone I could see eye-to-eye with, on account of we were the same height. Lunch was more of the same...fun.

Naturally, with three young boys to feed, John and my mother chose a nearby Italian restaurant with pizza on the menu. Really, do young boys eat anything other than pizza? No. They don't. So it was perfect, the five us sitting around one of those large, semi-circular booths ordering a pie. Me, my mom, Mackenzie, Mikey Walsh and Gomez Addams.

How Tall Are You?

Here's the thing about "celebrities". For some people in this country, a celebrity is someone who is thrust upon a pedestal, has some grand life where the streets are paved with gold and never-get-fat food. A mystical land where everyone loves them. Except their spouse. It isn't true. Celebrities are real people, with real problems and real, strange and sometimes gross encounters.

So there we were, the five of us, new friends, excited about the opportunity to be a part of something special, me super excited to be sitting next to Gomez Addams, and everything seemed...Normal. It could be that we were quite ready for lunch, and anyway who doesn't get excited about pizza? At least three fifths of our group, to be certain.

John Astin was the sweetest person. Nice, funny, accommodating to his children. Really, just another dad taking the kids to lunch. We could have been a family. Maybe the roads *were* paved in gold (or pepperoni). Maybe there *was* some grand pedestal where I belonged. My mom and Gomez Addams could have fallen in love. I could have had a pet hand. That mystical land where everyone loves me could have been mine. Mine!!! My precious!!!

Instead, when the pie got delivered, I reached my stubby little T-Rex arms across the table to get the parmesan shaker to make it rain cheesy goodness all over my pizza when I noticed something....not....right. Is that? A COCKROACH in the shaker?!?!??

Uh, garçon? Garçon! No pizza for us. How about a stale, dry turkey and not real cheese sandwich from a vending machine? The irony, of course, being that we had a horrible food experience while filming a music video to benefit child hunger in Africa. I'll contend, though, that food in your stomach doesn't do you any good if it makes you sick and ends up on the sidewalk a half hour later. I'm all for the 5 second rule when you drop your potato chip, but anytime roaches can make it into the cheese shaker, I'm thinking bigger issues loom large.

All that is to say, I would like to have seen the five of us exit that restaurant. You know the "gross dance" you do when something like this happens? A little bit robot dance, a little bit Elaine from Seinfeld, basically just limbs stretching out all over the place while a chill makes its way down your spine? That would have been us. Five of us walking out of the restaurant like dancing zombies. Michael Jackson would have been proud.

VIRGINIA

Dear Greg,
...I like your portrayal of Jamie King a lot.

Rosella R.
Charlottesville, VA

Dear Greg,
...I think you are cute.
P.S. I LOVE YOU!
Will you go with me?
How old are you?

Jennifer S.
Emporia, VA

Dear Greg,
Do you have a fan club. If you do how much does it
cost to join.

Alice T.
Petersburg, VA

How Tall Are You?

I laugh when I read things like someone liked my portrayal. I get the meaning. It's all about perspective. Fans think I was this thespian. A working Hollywood actor on a hit show on television. I thought I was a kid, being a kid. Oddly enough, I still portray a kid quite well, right down to the attention span and physical height. Of course now I have a beard, but that doesn't technically disqualify me from being a child. I could be in the circus, which wouldn't be wholly inappropriate.

Jennifer, from Emporia, wanted to go with me. I find it fascinating that she, like others, professed their love, then inquired about my age. That just proves that age is just a number. For the record, her letter was postmarked June of 1985, which would have made me twelve years old. Past my prime of peak cuteness.

I didn't have a fan club, nor do I now. How random would that be now? Ha ha ha. A whole fan club dedicated to an obscure actor from the 80s who really only had one hit. I love the idea, actually. We should make that happen. We just need a cute nickname for my fan. Or fans, if there are at least two of you out there.

Alice, you can join for free.

NO PROBLEM THERE, MOM

By 1987, my career in show business was winding down, but I had no idea at the time. Some things were out of my control, like the cancellation of Scarecrow and Mrs. King. Some things were of my own doing. Hubris, to some degree. I accept full responsibility for being a cocky little shit, it is the manner in which I've dealt with frustration, rejection and ultimately, bullying, my entire life. I own that.

It's just, well...The bullying.

Being a child actor, the one aspect I could have done without, unequivocally, is the bullying. You see, when kids are kids, they don't know how to deal with the roller coaster of emotions they feel. A big part of that confusion is communication. Kids don't know how to communicate they are confused about how they feel. They often hide it. For me, I hid my feelings in hubris. For others, they may lash out. For some, too many I think, they just regress into a self-imposed solitary confinement, robbing themselves of the pleasure of fellowship with other humans.

Kids don't communicate, so parents don't know what the hell is going on with them. Other kids, having problems of their own, don't know what the hell is going on with *them*. It's just a hormone fueled fuster-cluck that would be comedic, if it often wasn't so traumatic.

I started getting bullied in third grade. Most likely before that, but my earliest recollection of being bullied is from the third grade. I wasn't very big (I'm still not), was way too energetic for my own good, and I liked to entertain people, which meant I liked being the center of attention. The problem was, at eight years old, I didn't have an audience at school. The antics that killed in the living room at home, died on the blacktop at school. The other kids didn't like me for my talent, and I didn't know how to process that. I did what most kids do. I tried harder. It doesn't work.

Here's the rub...I'd do or say something to entertain, be the center of attention, and the other kids wouldn't like it. I'd try harder, and become *that* kid, and the kids would start to give me a hard time about it. I was acting like a kook, and getting called out for it. What's worse is when you act like a kook at school, the kids hate you for it, but then "that kid" gets rewarded with a chance to be on their television screens every Monday night at 8pm. Their parents watch, and maybe even say something like "Don't you go to school with that boy?" They're jealous of the attention, rightfully think I'm a kook, don't understand I just want to make people happy, that I want friends, and they undoubtedly have their own issues with school/friends/girls/boys/whatever. Many turn to bullying, the ancient art of tearing another person down to make yourself feel better.

Ripping me apart only fuels my desire to make you hate me more. If I can't entertain you, well then you're just going to be miserable with my success. As my brother can attest, I am a world class antagonizer. Why? Because you sure as hell aren't going to make me feel like I'm anything less than I'm not. I knew then, as I know now, that I can accomplish anything I set my mind to doing. I've seen the process work. It might take a while, and there might be failures along the way, but if I want something badly enough, it's going to happen.

Exception: I can't dunk a basketball. Try as I might, I can't defy physics. And believe me, I tried. Would you believe I used be to a fanatic for the game of basketball? I played several times a week for years. All day and night on the weekends. Especially during the summer. Turns out, I'm no Mugsy Bogues.

I digress. Subtracting any Newtonian laws that prevent me from taking my beloved Chicago Bulls to another World Championship, I can be who I want to be. Nobody is going to tell me different. Calling me short (a common theme during my years in school), four eyes, metal mouth, saying I have a large head or generally that I'm too much of a dork to be cool isn't really going to deter me from being me.

I'm definitely not going to be deterred if you refer to me as "fish sticks".

My last professional acting job was a nationally televised commercial for Van de Kamp's frozen fish, with Andrea Barber (Kimmy on Full House) who played my sister. The theme of the ad was that the fish are so fresh when they're frozen, they are practically still alive. Throughout the commercial, boxes of frozen fish come flying out of the grocery bag sitting in my lap. My last line, as I attempted to catch the flying boxes, was "No problem there, mom."

From that moment on, "fish sticks" became the go-to put-down when kids didn't like me.

I think I've been honest this whole book in saying that I know I was a little shit. Sometimes kids would've been right in giving me a hard time, because I could be a braggart. Most people know this as Little Man's Syndrome, where small guys tend to overcompensate in other areas of their lives. I was no different. And, honestly, when you take an offense approach to being bullied, one often becomes a bully themselves. Again, I was no different. I have a natural talent for finding a raw, open nerve in one's psyche and exploiting it, generally for the purpose of getting one to shut-the-hell-up. I'm not proud of this skill, mind you, and generally accept that most men have the ability to attack in this sort of manner. Men are often action first, thinking second.

Boys tend to epitomize this description. As mentioned, I had a talent for act first, think second. I don't justify my behavior at all. I'm not proud of the ability to zero in on a nerve. It is less who I am today than ever, not in small part to my wife. She was the first person outside of family to show me, truly, what love and acceptance are.

How Tall Are You?

I will say this, so that you clearly understand who I have always been. I can be a pretty easy going guy. My entire life I've been accepting of people and all their quirks. I learned early on that I was different than the other kids around me, but recognized that other kids were different too. I didn't belittle kids because of those differences. More often, I was fascinated by those differences. I do pride myself by having a wide variety of friends all through school. Sportos, motorheads, geeks, sluts, bloods, waistoids, dweebs, dickheads...It didn't matter to me. I was no Ferris Bueller, but you get the point. Where I got in trouble was if someone was being a jerk. I found some kids I went to school with felt they were better than others, and I often felt it my obligation to point out they weren't. A pacifist, I'm not.

If I was bullied or someone near me was bullied then my claws often came out. For a long time, I saw a lot of injustice in the world. I was high strung. Looking back, I realized being bullied affected me more that I put on. It had become important for me to prove to others that I was better, that I was right, that I wasn't what people said I was. I've struggled with seeing those injustices my entire life. Combine that with a confidence to say what I'm thinking to anyone, and well, it isn't necessarily a recipe for success every time.

My wife has taught me a lot.

I'm still not a fan of bullying. I think it is an epidemic in this country that isn't quite understood for the negative impact it has on our youth. It permeates our entire culture. I'm not necessarily an advocate for Political Correctness, either, but think our television programming is saturated with behavior that ultimately doesn't make us a better society. What many consider harmless, isn't. It's bullying. It's degrading others, and it's degrading society.

My belief in this is one reason why I'm so proud of the work we did on Scarecrow and Mrs. King. I think the show is removed from the pattern of bullying and insults. We put on a good show. It was a little corny, but it was fun. Ultimately, it was a safe environment for families to congregate and be entertained. Sure, we had some violence, but let's face it, people are violent toward each other. Anyway, violence was not the centerpiece to our show. It was good versus evil. And teamwork. That's a pretty awesome track record to have.

Honestly, it's taken me a long time to be genuinely proud of my work in the Van de Kamps television commercial. I've always cherished the experience of filming. Looking back, I'm disappointed the pressures of being on television, and the harassment and bullying that I endured happened at all. Emotionally, it forced me out of the entertainment business. It wasn't so much that I felt I couldn't defend myself against the naysayers anymore, it's that I was tired of doing so. I struggled with self-image and self-confidence, sure, but I was never at a breaking point. I'm fortunate that I persevered. Many kids don't. Especially many child actors.

What nearly broke me was the necessity of having to always be on the defensive at school. Which made me defensive at home. I have an older brother, who by all accounts was a typical older brother, not a bully, but by doing older brother things like tease and punch and whatever else older brothers do to lovingly torture their siblings, it forced me deeper into my cave of antagonizing arrogance. If anything, I probably bullied my brother more over the years than he has ever bullied me.

I never felt safe anywhere, free of criticism and ridicule.

The most disappointing part of all of this is that I didn't know that's what I was feeling, and was never able to communicate that with my family. They probably just thought I was a cocky little shit. Which, on the surface, was true. I never wanted to be that guy. It has taken me a very long time, and with a lot of heartache for me to finally see all of this.

Even then, it was my wife who has taught me the value of a safe place to be.

If I give it too much thought, I'm saddened that I didn't stay in entertainment. I think I could have had a lifelong career in it. Though, things work out for a reason. If I give it too much thought, I'm convinced that staying in entertainment through my high school years could have pushed me into a dark place emotionally. It is quite possible I could have been just another tragic case of child actor gone bad.

It's all speculation. There is a good chance I could have persevered longer than I thought, had my bumpy road through young adulthood and come out the other side as another Kurt Russell (It's my book, I can be whoever I want). I'm blessed with awesome parents. My dad has since passed away, but during my life was always an influential force. I don't doubt that he would have grabbed me by the scruff and hauled me off to a safe place had he seen me traveling down a dark path.

My mom, too. She was supportive of my decision to quit acting. She saw the challenges of rejection, of finding a job, the nature of some people to be one thing to your face and another behind your back. The entertainment industry doesn't have the reputation it has for no reason. In itself, the industry can be a bullying nightmare. It's quite possible my mom recognized already that I was having trouble at school. We've never discussed it.

My brother is a good man. He and I are in a great place. We struggled for many years, in part, I'm sure, because he experienced a lot of the same bullying I experienced. It isn't easy being the "TV star's brother". I didn't make it easy at home, and hell, it is just tough being a kid anyway. It took him a while to find out who he was. He lives out of state, and that makes me sad. When we're together now, even on the phone, it's safe. We still joke and insult each other, because, well, we're brothers, but it's different now. Being with him truly is a safe place to be.

I've dipped my toe back into the entertainment world a little over the years, even more so in recent years. I've become a different kind of storyteller, practicing my talent at writing books, screenplays, poetry and a blog online. My wife and I have an on again-off again podcast, and we've done several online videos. I have a 9-5 that keeps me engaged creatively, and even consists of some on-camera work. I recognize that my talents don't have to take me to Hollywood and a primetime television series for me to be successful.

The one question I get asked by those who know I was a child actor is "Would you go back to acting?" I would, if given the right opportunity. I'm not actively looking for jobs, but have spoken with people over the years. I guess if I really wanted it, I could have it. It's what I've always believed. I dream of it, but it isn't the most important thing in my life.

A safe place. I have that now, in no small part thanks to my wife. She's an incredible woman who has fought hard for our marriage, and for my mental well-being. You'd have to ask her, but I think she understood early in our relationship that I was a young man still searching for that safe place. It hasn't been easy finding it. Old habits. I still see a lot of injustice in the world, and find it difficult at times not to interject myself where I don't belong. I don't fancy myself a hero swooping in, but just fully understand my abilities to endure a bully. I haven't lost the confidence to speak my mind to anyone standing in front of me, but things are different now. Slower. I've developed the ability to *not listen*. It helps me avoid feeling compelled to verbally engage with the detractors.

My wife and I are a great team. She's an open, caring, sympathetic soul. I'm not. She is there for me when I need to be all of those things, and I'm there for her when she needs to be a little less so. She'd do just fine without my help, for sure, but every once in a while I do have to remind her that people are stupid.

In a version of my world, I'd have a private school just for child actors. Actually, I'd be surprised if they didn't already have this (I am aware of art schools). Anyway, part of their education would be social participation. The curriculum would consist of recognizing bullying and teaching interaction with people who don't understand the difference between artist and art. Also, it would teach young actors how not to be little shits. Maybe we'd need a class for parents, too.

If I had to do it all over again, knowing what I know now? The age old dream, right? Yeah, I'd do things differently. But I don't waste time on that dream. I love my life. I have a great partner in life who is also a great teacher (and great student). I have amazing kids that I can teach these lessons I've learned, in hopes they don't make the same mistakes I did. So far, so good. My family loves me, and I love them.

Life doesn't get any better than that.

WASHINGTON D.C.

Dear Greg Morton

...Would you please personally write, in ink on this card I've enclosed - To Maurice from Greg Morton - and I will put it in my book. I will keep it, and be grateful. I know you won't let me down.

Mr. Maurice S.
Washington D.C.

No extra card remains in the envelope, so...Success? Mr. Maurice was quite polite, which I appreciate but, let's face it, laid the guilt on a little heavy there, no? Apparently, I'm a sucker for polite guilt, as there wasn't an extra card left in the envelope and Maurice didn't write me repeatedly over the years.

Why do I have a Steve Miller song stuck in my head?

ONE FLEW EAST

I'm convinced that in 1984, the producers of the show wanted to kill my mom.

I mean, really, what is the one thing you want to do with a hyper eleven year old boy? Put him on a plane for thirteen hours or more! Seems logical, right?

I'm sure the 1984 Summer Olympics, when hundreds of thousands of people had descended on Los Angeles for two weeks effectively making it impossible to film any location shots, had *nothing* to do with Scarecrow and Mrs. King packing up its bags and heading for Europe. It could very well be they wanted to punish my mom for ever unleashing me onto the world, and thought countless hours inside of a metal toothpaste tube at thirty thousand feet might do the trick. I'm sure if you asked my mom, she'd concede they were correct.

On any account, Germany bound we were, for fourteen days. And instead of just making this a working trip, my dad and my brother tagged along to make it a working family vacation. Lucky them. They got to spend the nearly six hour flight from Los Angeles to New York in Coach, while my mom and I enjoyed First Class. Ditto for the flight to Germany. Being part of a television show has its perks, but not if you asked my brother.

If it makes anyone feel better, that Germany trip was the only time I've ever flown First Class. Like most of society, when I fly I have to pass by the First Class seats when boarding a plane like a nineteenth century street urchin begging for scraps in an Off-Off-Broadway production of Oliver. It always seems like a Monty Python sketch to me, the First Classers spilling their champagne as they snicker and laugh at the Never-Weres. Of course, on an international flight one takes a 747 where the cabin door is more center fuselage, and thus First Class is a left turn when you board the plane while all others are a right turn. Basically, I missed my chance to be a pretentious snob and look down upon those in Coach. Like my dad and brother.

My memory of the flight to Germany was that it was long. I know, right? That's in-depth knowledge you just can't get anywhere else, folks. My point is, there was really nothing special about that flight. At that time, I'd flown several times in my life. One of my most memorable flights prior to 1984 was the day my family moved from Cincinnati, Ohio to Los Angeles in August of 1979. That flight, probably around 4 hours or so, was memorable, in most part because of the weather but also because the move itself was life changing. From the Midwest to the West Coast doesn't happen very often.

Heading to Germany, we left LAX and flew into La Guardia Airport in New York for the first leg of our flight, and then had to change plans in N.Y. To set the scene, for those of you who haven't made such a trip, imagine walking through an airport, and then sitting and waiting around for a while before you board your plane so that you can sit and wait around for a while longer on the flight itself, only to de-plane and walk through an airport so you can sit and wait for a bit before boarding another plane and then...sit and wait.

It's a lot of sitting. Sadly, people watching, and more importantly the pleasure I derive from such activity, wasn't a skill I had developed at eleven years old or that would have made the trip more enjoyable. Instead, I was numbingly bored. Excited to be going on a trip. But bored. In New York I was just a third of the way through my day of boredom, so there was that.

How Tall Are You?

Enter First Class. Luxurious seats, plenty of space, an entire section of people that realized they just entered into a ten hour commitment with a helmet headed motormouth. That would be me. I'm sure if Prozac was as prevalent then as it is now, the flight attendants would have offered it as a gesture of mercy.

So, how does an eleven year old occupy himself on a ten hour flight? Talk. Fidget, fuss, complain, make endless trips to the bathroom. Talk some more. Which wasn't great for everyone else considering we were on an overnight flight. People were trying to sleep, you know? Not that it concerned me, mind you. I was too busy talking.

If you asked my mom, she would tell you I wasn't that bad. This, of course, is if you asked her today. Like the pain of childbirth, the pain of our flight is most likely something my mother has forgotten. Who could blame her?

There remain two distinct memories I have of the flight over the Atlantic. First, the ocean. It is wide and it is vast and no matter how many times you look out of the window on a flight from New York, USA to Munich Germany, it is always underneath you. I found that both peaceful, and alarming. I mean, seriously, how does the pilot know where he/she is going if they don't have a landmark? That is the whole point of a LAND-mark! Must be all of those dials and things they have in the cockpit. Remember, this was eleven year old me. But that's not to say I'm not still in awe of Trans-Atlantic navigation.

My other memory was the man seated next to me across the aisle who, out of sheer pity for my mom no doubt, taught me a card trick. It blew my mind when he pulled the trick on me, about three times, before finally offering the magician's reveal. I still remember how to do the trick, but I must confess it probably works best on eleven year olds trapped inside a PVC pipe hurling across the sky.

Once we landed in Germany, my mom recalls that I was patted down by security as we made our way through customs, and that, most notably, I wasn't happy about being touched. I'm rather amused by this story. Mom didn't say, but I can only imagine that I said something to the security guard. Classic little guy.

In the years since I've traveled often and, on occasion, have had to be screened separately by security. I think it's my beard. Security either doesn't believe that someone so short, seemingly a child to their eyes, could grow such magnificence or they just want a closer look. That being said, security personnel has patted me down as an adult, and still I find it amusing. In part because they tend to look more uncomfortable than I feel. I'm never pleased I'm getting sequestered for an additional check, but they have a job to do and as long as I don't miss my flight I'm golden. Besides, who wouldn't want to get closer to my magnificent beard?

I know, I know...What does any of this have to do with Scarecrow and Mrs. King? The answer? Absolutely nothing. In truth, any memory I have of our trip to Germany has little, if anything to do with the show. All told my mom and I were there for fifteen days, and of that I worked two. Admittedly not a bad gig if you can get it.

However, I was on call for the entire time I was there, which meant we weren't hopping a train for sexy locales like Zurich, Milan or Prague. Not that Munich isn't sexy. It is. In 1984, I found Munich to be exceptionally clean, the people quiet, reserved and polite, and the McDonalds in town had beer on the menu. Sexy, no?

We did travel around a bit, mostly in town. We took a day trip to the Bavarian town of Oberammergau, nestled among the hills at the foot of the Alps. We traveled by train, my first trip by such method, and arrived back in time to a village that had all of the culture and charm of old world Bavaria. Oberammergau is widely known for its history of presenting the Passion Play, a fact not lost on my mother, I'm sure. I was eleven, so religious theater and wood carvings, another art form the town is famous for, was almost completely lost on me.

I was in awe of the landscape. It felt like my childhood fantasies of conquering dragons or beast in far off lands had all taken place in a setting like Oberammergau. It was almost surreal. The mountains, the bright blue sky, the greenery everywhere you looked. By this time in our overall trip I was wearing a Tyrolean hat everywhere I went and, traveling with Paul, his mom and siblings I'm sure I fancied myself the leader of an American expedition of risk and adventure. Which, to be sure, traveling with me, my brother, Paul and his brothers there was risk and adventure for all parents involved.

I have no doubt that while I was day dreaming some medieval band of explorers into new worlds of discovery, Kate and Bruce and all of the others from the show were probably working. Cast, crew. Everyone. Working hard at putting on a television show. You know, earning their paychecks.

I worked too, when I wasn't playing. Two days. We filmed scenes for the episode The Times They Are A Changin', mostly in and around the Marienplatz, home to the world famous Glockenspiel. Real difficult work. Pretend I'm a tourist taking pictures of a famous clock. Done! Cut. Wrap.

I do recall that as an American television production in a foreign country, we didn't enjoy the same luxuries of location that we'd enjoy back home. Mainly, the ability to sequester a set. That is to say, we weren't able to tell folks "Hey, you. Yeah, you. You live here, right? Great! Go away. We want to film and, we don't want you in our shot."

It doesn't happen quite so rudely, but that's the main idea. If we aren't paying for your face, we don't want your face. What ends up happening, and you can really see it in the scenes at the Marienplatz, is a crowd full of people looking directly into the camera. Smooth, guys. Real smooth. *THAT'S* not obvious or anything.

How Tall Are You?

For the initial shot of Amanda, Dotty, Phillip and Jamie all gazing up at the Glockenspiel and I'm taking photos (and making some of the most awesome faces I've ever made on screen), we were surrounded by "our people" so that the oogling crowd couldn't be seen. It's the reason we are so packed in like sardines.

Movie Magic!

The Marienplatz was an awesome place to hang out for a few days. I highly recommend. My memories of that time are specific to the waitresses serving steins of beer by the fistful, in a feat that can only be attributed to them being badass. It is both a skill and an art form.

Second is the photograph I took of Bruce Boxleitner. "The Picture" as it is known in my family (by my mom really) perfectly captured a handsome, young Bruce out in the wild. As I made my way through the crowds of the Marienplatz taking pictures of just about anything, I had spied Bruce through the crowd and, noticing that I was about to take his picture he leaned for the perfectly framed shot. A good photograph is as much subject as it is photographer.

How Tall Are You?

Overall, my German experience was a tourist trip, and uneventful until the trip home. We were asked to stay an extra day for a press junket, but my dad and my brother had to fly home as scheduled. My mom was uneasy about being in a foreign country without my dad, but hey...What could go wrong?

It turned out that everything went as scheduled in country. We did the press junket, and made our flight out the next day. Into a building storm on the eastern seaboard of the United States. Our return trip was, naturally, a reverse of our trip out to Germany. Munich to La Guardia to LAX. Easy peasy.

Remember, it was a ten hour flight across the Atlantic? Yeah, I remember that too. It is a long time to be stuck on a plane. And then, just when you think you're getting close, the captain comes on and says the flight is being re-routed to Newark, New Jersey because of the storm. Soon, your flight begins to get...Longer.

We couldn't get into Newark. It was either the storm itself or the backlog from all of the New York flights. I think we were in a holding pattern while the people on the ground figured it out, which I'm sure was no picnic. Imagine having to slot planes into locations in a hurry knowing you've got hundreds of people flying around above you. Air traffic controllers do an amazing job and is mostly a thankless job, in my opinion.

Anyway, both La Guardia and nearby Newark were out. So now what? Good ole Washington Dulles Airport, Washington D.C. Home of the nation's capital, and the setting for a little show about spies called Scarecrow and Mrs. King. Hours after we were supposed to land in New York, we touched down in the District.

Only to sit on the plane for at least another four hours.

There was so much diverted traffic that we were lucky enough to land, but there weren't any available terminals for us to pull into. And I mean we were lucky. We sat on the tarmac in the pouring rain for hours, which meant more flights were being diverted away from D.C. We could have still been in the air looking for some real estate.

We finally got off the plane after having spent nearly a full day inside. Not that our ordeal was over at that point, because now we were just several of hundreds that were stranded far from their intended destination. Luckily for my mom, we were with Deena, Paul and Paul's brothers, Scott and Ricky.

How Tall Are You?

Of course, now, there we were. Two moms, four kids, hundreds of other stranded travelers dumped off in an airport in the middle of the night after having to sit on planes for God knows how many hours. A lot. A lot of hours.

The bathrooms in the airport had lines, which, isn't necessarily out of the ordinary if you're a woman, which, to be honest, I don't understand. Is it just because the process takes longer, there is more undressing involved versus a zip-and-go or what? Nevermind. Forget I asked. I think I'm better off not knowing. Women have it rough in the toilet department, no doubt. I'll stop now.

The bathroom had lines. So did the bar, which was remarkable only in that the bars were the only establishment in the airport open at that time of night. Pretty much every poor soul that had gotten off of our plane (or any plane, for that matter) hadn't eaten since the Mid-Atlantic, and so we were all a little...Hangry. That's hungry+angry. Hangry.

Ok, so I was hangry. I'm sure everyone else in our little party wasn't quite so attitudinal. There are two things I don't handle very well; Lack of food and lack of sleep.

Lucky for my mom and everyone else, I was short on both. Honestly, I may be exaggerating about the hangry thing. Because I was so tired, I may have hallucinated that. Seriously.

I was so tired that I fell asleep standing up.

I didn't think that was possible, but, ta-da! Not movie magic, mind you, but severely sleep deprived little boy with a desire to NEVER SIT AGAIN. I'd been on the plane too long, and sitting was about the last thing I'd wanted to do. Ever. I'm rather dramatic. Writing all of this out, it occurs to me I might be a diva. Now I'm trying to decide if I run with that or keep it in the closet. I digress.

There wasn't much mom or Deena could do about the bathrooms. We all had to take our turns standing in line or watching luggage. The girls did their thing, the boys all did theirs. Once that mission had been accomplished, it was time for food. Since the bar was the only thing open, the moms were the only ones that could really facilitate food requisition. They being of age to walk into a bar, and of course they being the only two with money that wasn't a couple of folded up Deutsche Marks.

Us boys had all found a spot next to a pillar that wasn't occupied by the throngs, and set up shop. I have no doubt Paul and others et al were spread out across the floor like wrapping paper at Christmas. Me? I stood, leaning against the pillar. I wasn't about to sit. I'd been sitting. I'd had my fill. Nobody could force me to sit.

Diva.

I specifically remember that body-shake-awake thing you do when you're exhausted and fall into a deep sleep for, like, fifteen seconds. In class. Your body jolts you awake as if to say "Hey, stupid, the teacher just called your name. WAKE UP!" That was me at the airport. I fell asleep, jerked myself awake, realized I was standing and then...my knees buckled. Luckily, I don't have far to fall to the ground.

Just as I was lifting my sorry carcass up from the floor, mom and Deena arrived with "dinner". Quotes are necessary at this juncture, because quite frankly I'm playing it fast and loose with the term dinner. The two moms and four underage boys noshed on stale hot dogs and beer for dinner. Allegedly.

How Tall Are You?

Allegedly there wasn't anything else to drink besides beer, and allegedly in my mind I remember the beer being room temperature and flat. Which would have been appropriate since we'd just arrived from Europe. I'm kidding, of course. The beer would have, allegedly, been disgusting because I was eleven years old.

All of this allegedly business because I don't want to get my mom in any kind of trouble (30+ years later). In her defense, though, they were in survival mode. We were all cold, tired and hungry. The airport was socked in with rain. It was like the Donner Party. My mom fed me stale hot dogs and beer. Allegedly. If anything, she's been punished already. I'm sure I complained. A lot.

Of course, all of this and we were stuck in an airport, three thousand miles from home. My mom's future consisted of more lines as she waited for a pay phone to call my dad, just to update him on our whereabouts. This was pre-internet, my friends. Pre-mobile phones. This was when folks had to be resourceful about things. She had to make a call, then hang up, coordinate with Deena, and then stand in line again to make another call. It was brutal. I'm not a huge fan of our dependence on cell phones, but the lines for everything at Dulles Airport that night were brutal.

It turns out, we'd be stuck for nearly two days. The only flights out of D.C. to Los Angeles were through St. Louis, and even then it was a layover situation. With storms still affecting the east coast and mid-west, my mom didn't want to risk it. Somehow, she and Deena were able to score two hotel rooms, and even more remarkably, two cabs. We'd be staying the night in the District.

It turns out, the delay wasn't all that bad, from my perspective. Deena had a relative in nearby Virginia that picked us up the next day and drove us around D.C. We saw the changing of the guard at the Tomb of the Unknown Soldier at Arlington Cemetery. We got stopped in traffic and saw President Reagan's motorcade go speeding right by us. I didn't see the president, but I saw the car. Or cars, as it were.

That night, we had a fried chicken dinner at Deena's relative's house, and all of us boys chased fireflies out in the yard.

The next day we flew out on a non-stop flight to Los Angeles. It had taken us three days, but we'd finally made it back home from Munich. The first thing my dad and brother did when they picked us up from the airport was take us out for pizza. A grand celebration for returning home, if I do say so myself.

It was an ordeal, but our trip to Germany was the right kind of eventful. It's not an adventure until something goes wrong. We got the trip of a lifetime, and got paid to do it. Like I've said, admittedly not a bad gig if you can get it.

WEST VIRGINIA

Greg,

...I think you are a good actor.

.I'm 13 years old ...+ think you're <u>really</u> cute!...

...If you ever get this write me + give me your real phone # + address.

P.S. I would really like to see you sometime.

Aaron C.
St. Albans, WV

Dear Greg,

...I love to watch Scarecrow and Mrs. King it is my favorite show!

...I think you are cute and I would like to have your autographed picture.

Love (from your no. 1 (hopefully) fan)
Jennifer G.
Lewisburg, WV

How Tall Are You?

I'm still humbled by letters from girls that thought I was cute. I was, at one point. It is undeniable. That first year on the show...Lookout! But as the years progressed...Lookout! And not in a good way. I've mentioned it before, just re-watch Season 3 or 4 episodes and you'll see a kid with ridiculously strong neck muscles, because that's the only way one would account for being able to hold up such a large head. You'd think that with small feet, a short torso and monster sized melon that I'd fall over a lot.

In writing this book, I've re-read all of these letters, word for word, to select what gets shared and to reminisce. When I re-read Aaron's letter, I didn't know if I was reading a letter from a boy or girl. That wasn't what bothered me. What bothered me is that Aaron wanted my real phone number and address. Sheesh...So pushy.

I'm kidding. It is a little forward, but sure, you can have all of my personal information. Back then it may not have been the kind of issue it would be in this digital age. Still, no. Ha ha.

Going back to whether Aaron is a boy or girl, I've deduced the letter was from a girl. But I have to be honest, I was kind of hoping it was a boy. How cool would it have been back in 1986 for a young boy to be that comfortable with himself to write his feelings to another boy? I know this may be a touchy subject for some, but, well...get over it. There are real problems in this world, and people loving other people isn't one of them.

There are kids in the United States, *this country*, that don't know where their next meal is coming from. *Kids*. When we've solved that issue, I'll eagerly hear any argument anyone would like to make on any subject. Until then, shut it down.

I'll step off my box, now. I did kind of like it up there, though. Must be what tall people feel like. Tall.

Anyway, thanks Aaron, for writing. Even if you are a girl.

Jennifer wrote, too. I'm not sure if she is my number one fan, but for shits & giggles let's just say she is. Get that girl a name badge!

ALL THAT GLITTERS

"I don't have to tell you my name, you know my name. I've been here lots of times and you've never hired me."

That was a me quote. Nice, huh? I've been saying for a whole book now that I was a little shit, but you didn't believe me, did you? Come on...Be honest.

Remember when I said I didn't have a problem speaking my mind to anyone? Yeah, well, that tradition started early. Like, as a pre-teen auditioning for parts on television. I definitely said the above quote once, but probably thought it a million times. This particular gem got me in trouble with my agent.

Casting agents routinely have to see thousands and thousands of clients for work, and many of them children. Imagine that, thousands of child actors, with stage parents. Not a job I would want, for sure. Sometimes it's tough enough being in line behind some rambunctious offspring of the frayed hair, disheveled, glassy eyed mom in front of me at the market, tugging on her shirt saying "Mom, mom, mom, mom, mom, mom..."

Aaaaarrrrgggghhhhh!!!!!!

If that kid was standing in front of me for a job? Ha ha ha, yeah, no. Now, to be clear, I wasn't that bad. It was never my intention to be disrespectful, and I certainly wasn't going to be rude. My parents didn't raise me that way, and besides, my parents are also old-school. I most certainly would have had my ass handed to me if I was ever too out of line. If you haven't gotten the sense already, let me be clear now, my parents didn't care if I was on television or not. If I was acting like a serious fool, they would have pulled me away from acting and dropped me off at the nearest military academy for kids who need a boot in their camp, pronto.

I was a pill at times. But more like a gummy vitamin. I'm better than a nightcap of Nyquil, but not quite as sweet as a real gummy.

Still, the above quote almost got me unrepresented by my Agency. It seems the casting agent called my talent agent, and my talent agent called my Agent of Discipline:

Mom. I was promptly told that if I ever did that again, they wouldn't represent me. I got the point. Sort of.

I was sixteen the last time I auditioned for a job on television. I remember the afternoon I drove myself out to the city, in traffic, by myself, a microwave sized mobile phone taking up most of the passenger seat of my Honda. Seriously. Ever see those old war movies when the captain wants to talk with command so he yells at the private carrying this huge backpack that has a regular phone receiver on it? That was basically my first mobile phone, sans the energetic private dodging bullets so I could call my mom.

Anyway, the last audition was for a commercial, I don't remember the specifics. Not that it matters, as I walked in with no desire to audition, no desire to perform, no desire to be that dancing monkey. It no doubt showed. I called my agent after the audition, and that was it. I'd had it with acting. I was done. It wasn't the best, most professional phone call I've ever made.

It wasn't that I was rude, it's that I wasn't a professional. Professionals work. Especially in this business, because just finding work is tough enough. The ones who take it seriously will work some jobs that aren't their first choice so they can be recognizable for the jobs that are.

By this time in my life, I was over Hollywood. I wanted the jobs I wanted, but...Well. There was a lot going on. Scarecrow and Mrs. King, for me, had ended abruptly. I had been riding high on having a steady job. It was easier to work and be noticed when you had that kind of exposure. And then, I was just another cow in the stable looking for a bale of hay. At a time in my life when self-esteem was probably at its most vulnerable, I was struggling to find my way.

Balance.

Oh, sure, I know all about Balance now. But I'm thirty (cough, cough) or so years removed from being fully engaged with the entertainment business. Sixteen year old me didn't know there was a light at the end of that tunnel. At the time, things just seemed to be getting darker. Hollywood, for me, had lost that glitter.

It's an old trope, really. Not all that glitters is gold. Stories abound how Hollywood eats people up. In reality, Hollywood as a town isn't all that glamorous. Much like movie magic on the big screen, people in this town only show you the good stuff, like an Instagram feed. The entertainment industry is tough, and you've got to be tough. Rejection sucks, and I'd had my fill.

Getting back to that phone conversation with my agent, I'm fairly confident it was a relief for her to hear I was done. My recollection is a tad fuzzy, but I'm certain I traveled down the "I'm better than commercials, I want to do movies" road. Which, when you say things like that, means that you aren't better. You're just a pill. Maybe a gummy vitamin, but borderline a dry, chalky, tastes like bitter cement horse-pill that gets stuck in the back of your throat when you try to wash it down.

I'd been auditioning for a while and just not getting any jobs. The challenge was trying to juggle school, homework, after school activities like sports, friends and family with driving forty miles across town on freeways more crowded than a Walmart on Black Friday. For a teenager, it was easy to throw in the towel on the acting thing when I had so many other things closer to home. It wasn't necessarily the right choice, but it was the easy choice.

In truth, I'd experienced this level of frustration for quite some time. During my time on Scarecrow and Mrs.

King, I would continue to audition for other parts. Often, I would audition the same day as filming a scene for the show. In many cases, filming for me only took a couple of hours, in the morning. My calls were early, then we'd film, most likely I'd have to do required schooling, then the producers would release us for the day.

On those days, my mom would call into my agent, who often had me booked for an audition in the afternoon. Hollywood proper is a small town, but show business is spread out all over the greater Los Angeles area. Also, we filmed at the Burbank Studios (now called Warner Bros. Studios). Auditions could be near Burbank or they could be a few miles away in Studio City or Hollywood or across town on the west side like Santa Monica or Venice.

We could drive a half hour to an hour to get to an audition in the late afternoon just to be there five minutes. One time, in an audition in Venice, a beach town on the west side where parking is notoriously bad, my mom dropped me off for my audition and drove around the block looking for parking. When she pulled around the corner for another pass, I was already standing outside on the curb, audition complete. I was the only one they were seeing, and apparently the role didn't call for a four foot tall child with an exceptionally large head but no chin.

How Tall Are You?

We lived in the suburbs, and so the problem with auditioning in a place like Venice was that it was another thirty miles in the opposite direction of home. After an early call on SMK, then a drive out to an audition, we'd then have to drive seventy miles back home in infamous L.A. traffic. All of this was easy when I was a co-pilot and mom was doing all of the driving.

Once I became of age to drive myself - Ugh. No thanks. I didn't need to be driving clear across town for some guy who couldn't remember my name after a million visits to reject me out of hand because I wasn't cute anymore or wasn't tall enough or didn't have blue eyes or couldn't read the script well enough to sell the company's widget. Just so I could get stuck in mind numbing traffic on the way home.

In hindsight, I should have returned to the stage, where I had essentially started my career. I think it would have been easier for me to find the rewarding work that I desperately wanted, but it would have also forced me back to being a little more disciplined. The stage is more demanding than the screen in many ways. The highs and lows are immediate. Stage actors practice until they drop, sure, you have to, because when the house lights dim, you have to know your part. There is no calling for line when you're in the middle of a scene on stage and an audience is waiting for you to deliver. Waiting for you to entertain.

I think that I missed the risk involved with the stage. Not so much that I didn't love filming television or commercials, but by that point in my development as a human being I was such an emotional dumpster fire, the fear and adrenaline of stage work would have been cathartic. This is all hindsight, of course.

Writing has become my catharsis. The risk isn't quite the same, not as immediate, but it allows for reflection. When I write these things out, it becomes easier for me to see myself from the outside. I think being a pill was natural to some degree. My level of arrogance was mild compared to some of the real experiences I've had with actors, and stories I've heard of others. I think my behavior was natural, and necessary. Not for the world, of course. The world doesn't need another little twit. Turn on the news these days and anyone can discover that.

No, I think my attitude was a natural progression for me. A learning curve. It wasn't my intention for this chapter to turn into another soliloquy on bullying or my mental state as a child actor, but I guess that's where it's taken me. Hollywood isn't all glamorous, and that can be especially difficult for a child.

The years following my time on Scarecrow and Mrs. King were...Rough. I had a difficult time adjusting to "real life", whatever that is. The bullying didn't stop, my attitude didn't get any better, and I was basically looking for acceptance. I wanted people to see how cool I really was, even though I wasn't.

My first year in high school I was totally lost.

Looking back now, I realize I had no direction. Early in the school year I tried out for the freshman football team because my best friend at the time tried out too. Freshman football is the team they let everyone wear a uniform or, at least, that's what it seemed like. There is no reason a five foot tall, top heavy wondermunchkin should be allowed in a battle zone with kids twice his size clad in helmets and suffering from teen angst. It could be the coaches understood we were *all* suffering from teen angst, and a little violence would do us some good. Who knows? Not this guy.

Needless to say, freshman football wasn't a success. They put the short kid out as wide receiver. I was fast, and that could be a reason they put me there, but I think mostly I was there because I would have gotten creamed anywhere near the line. Honestly, football was never my thing. To make matters worse for me, the coach's kid played first string and I thought I was better. I wasn't, but my ego didn't know that.

I got put into one game. Ran the wrong route. The QB tossed the ball to another player. I got pulled from the game. I was a sideline grunt from then on, until I got kicked off the team for failing to make grades. Definitely a low point.

I wasn't good with girls. I wasn't good in sports. I wasn't good in class. Add to my frustrations unruly hair, glasses, braces, acne and hormones. I was like a John Hughes movie, but without all of the humor, charm, or Molly Ringwald.

There is a part of me that understands how easy it is for child actors to get into trouble. With drugs. With sex. With the wrong people. I understand how difficult childhood can be for kids in general. The wrong road can be easy to travel when you're trying to discover who you are. As a culture, I don't think we pay enough attention to that time in our lives. Certainly not as parents. I believe that discovery is essential, in a supportive environment, and too many adults dismiss it with a wave of the hand.

Communication by all parties involved is a huge obstacle to overcome. Parents don't know what the kids are really thinking because the kids aren't telling them, in large part because the kids have no idea what the hell is going on with them anyway. I didn't talk to my parents. I hid my feelings, not understanding truly what they were.

I didn't have anyone in my life that understood me. Not my best friend, not my parents, not my brother. Four people, mind you, were all I felt I had in the world, and not a single one knew I was spiraling into an emotional abyss. Some people at that age are surrounded by scores of people, some are truly alone. I was in the in-between.

I started this book by telling you I'm dreamer.

I have no doubt that being a dreamer saved my life. I reached a low point of self-esteem and aimless questioning of my purpose in life. I was lost. In being lost, I learned the only way to find my way back was to get lost. To let go. To lose myself in music, in books, in film.

In dreams.

How Tall Are You?

I don't recall the first time I sat to write a poem. At the time it was most likely to write a song (or a rap song, as it were) more so than a poem. Even today I'd describe my poetry as an attempt at song lyrics. When I started, it was just a way to express myself. It was a world where anything was possible, where I could be anything I wanted to be, without fear of competition or criticism.

Writing poetry led me to writing a blog, in the beginning mostly about music, and then ultimately, to writing books. I began experimenting with digital design, after a lifetime of sketching. My path led me to a degree in graphic design, then a creative career in design, marketing and finally, back to film. My work now is on a completely different scale than being on a hit network television show, but my path has been found. I have been found.

I belong in the creative arts.

I continue to write, both books, blog posts (on occasion) and screenplays. I've given one of my screenplays to friend (and former Scarecrow and Mrs. King producer) Dennis Duckwall. His notes were positive and encouraging. It's a start. I'm also helping support friends who are independent artists, both in music and in film. I try to keep in touch with my fan-base, and share the awesome creative talent I come across. I'm still a dreamer. I have a million ideas (on paper and in my head) of new stories to tell. I'm working at getting them out there to share with fans.

I've realized that I would love a second chance at being in front of the camera again, if for no other reason than to see if I could do it. Certainly if they were to ever revive Scarecrow and Mrs. King, you can be sure I'd sign on.

For now, I'll keep forging my own path. I'll keep writing poems, writing fiction, maybe even write another non-fiction book after this one. There's a great big world out there, and I think there's room enough for me and my work.

I guess now if I were to drop a "Do you know who I am?" line on someone, the answer would be...A Hollywood survivor.

WISCONSIN

Dear Greg,

I enjoy watching Scarecrow and Mrs. King.

Jennifer A.

Sussex, WI

Dear Gerg,

...Are you 11 years old? I watch your show when I can. Sometimes I don't get to watch your show. It is petty nice people can write to you.

JoAnn G.

Mondovi, WI

Jennifer's letter was short, but long enough to mention she lived near Milwaukee. I probably lived there the same length of time it took her to write her letter.

JoAnn's letter was dated September 17th, 1985, so...No, Joann, I was not eleven years old. I was twelve. And a half.

How Tall Are You?

I don't think it's petty that nice people can write. It's petty to point out you spelled my name wrong.

On a side note, there were a dozen cigarette papers folded up in the letter that JoAnn sent. Unused. I'll leave it to you to figure that one out.

CANADA

Dear Greg,

...I watch Scarecrow and Mrs. King all the time hoping I'll see you. I think you and Paul should get a better storyline.

...I'm 5"5...

Alot of kids in showbussiness are stuck-up nerds and don't give a hoot. I hope you're not like that.

Tammy B.
Montreal, Quebec

Dear Greg,

...I think you are an extremely good actor. "Scarecrow" is my number #1 _favorite_ show.

...Please tell me all about yourself like, what your favorite show is? hobbies? Sports?

P.S. Please say Hi to Kate, Bruce, Paul and Beverly. Tell them who sent it. Thanks.

Stephen G.
Calgary, Alberta

How Tall Are You?

Dear Greg Moton,

...I like you as Jamie King on Scarecrow and Mrs King.

...How do you like working with Kate Jackson as your Tv mom is she fun to work with.

April Z.
Burlington, Ontario

I'm totally not a stuck-up nerd. Ask me. Just don't interrupt me when I'm reading a Brief History of Time at Spago's while waiting for my order of foie gras and caviar. Or whatever the hell it is that stuck-up nerds do. Ok, clearly I don't know.

Tammy, dear Tammy. You were 12 when you wrote in 1985. It took me another six or seven years to reach your height, and by then I could drive. My guess is you play on the women's national volleyball team by now. Or are a tree.

And apparently my name in Canadian French translates to "Morgan", as that was who the envelope was addressed to.

How Tall Are You?

Stephen wrote a year earlier, in 1984. Magnum P.I. was my favorite show in 1984. Hawaii, short shorts, a red Ferrari 308 GTS and the manliest mustache of all time. Who *wasn't* a fan of that show?!?

I don't know much about Canada, but I was under the impression that Quebec was where the French Canadians were located, and thus the bulk of non-English speaking Canadians. Having never been to Ontario, I'm curious what language translated my name to "Moton".

I appreciate my international fans, I really do. In large part because their stamps cost more to reach me. It's an investment to write someone. Especially someone like me.

It makes me wonder, though. Do you think April ever wrote to Kate and asked *her* what it was like working with me?

I bet Kate would have said something like "Working with Greg is great. I have only nice things to say because I feel one day he is going to write a book, and I'm going to be in it."

How Tall Are You?

If she was being honest, she'd inquire how one kid could manage the additional weight of braces and glasses on such a bulbous head and not fall over more often.

I'd say working with Kate was like a dream come true.

FAST FOOD for THOUGHT

You've gotten through this book and thought "What the hell, you haven't written a single word about Mel Stewart?!"

Truth is, I don't have any great Mel stories. In fact, I really don't have *any* Mel stories. We were almost never on set together, and when we were, I did my best not to bug him (of which I have a particular skill-set). Mel never treated me any way but friendly and with respect. He was known for a gruff exterior, and for speaking his mind. Why wouldn't he? He was a seasoned professional, a serious musician, a working actor. I'm sure he didn't have time for some freckled clod known for entertaining the crew by break dancing on the living room floor.

Not that Mel didn't have a sense of humor or wasn't a fun guy. I'm just not the one to tell you those stories. Wait for when Martha Smith ever writes a book. Or ask Bruce at an autograph show to tell you a Mel story. Those stories are better when they're in those voices anyway. What you'll get from me is that Mel intimidated the hell out of me every time I saw him because he'd give me a stern look. Just a look. That look like you know the man standing in front of you knows everything about what you've done and what you are about to do in life and don't think for one minute you'd be able to con him with some cheap card trick you learned on a plane once. It just wouldn't happen.

I have no doubt he knew he intimidated me, too. He most likely got a chuckle out of it. I do know he had a great sense of humor. I can still remember seeing him laugh and his face would light up.

There's a reason they hired him to be THE GUY at the Agency to oversee agents. It wasn't just that he projected steely resolve and smarts. That *was* Mel. Smart.

***

Sam Melville played my dad on the show. I discovered years later, in my thirties, that Sam had done a surf film called Big Wednesday. It is widely considered the closest Hollywood has ever gotten to capturing the true heart of surfers and surf culture, especially for the time. I began surfing as an adult, and when I saw the movie I remember feeling depressed to some degree. Sam had been gone years by then, taken way too early at the age of 52 in 1989, and I'd never gotten a chance to talk to him about this film.

The difficult thing about being a child actor is that you don't have anything in common yet with the adults you work with. They're adults...You're not. For me, growing into adulthood opened my eyes to a world I could discuss with my acting peers, to use the term loosely. By then, though, I was no longer a peer.

With Sam, it wouldn't have mattered anyway. We lost him before I was an adult. His death still bothers me. Like the missed opportunity to give one last hug to Beverly, there's an emptiness when I think about Sam. It wasn't like we were close, but, for a moment, he made an impact.

Sam Melville has the humorous distinction of playing a role as a guest star on Scarecrow and Mrs. King, and then returning to the show to play my father, Joe King, in four episodes. I remember meeting him in the living room set on Stage 24. He was warm, friendly and soft spoken. Sam was another of those handsome, manly guys, like Bruce. When he walked on set, there was a buzz about him.

I only remember him to be kind and attentive. And he smelled like a man should. I know that sounds weird, but that's what I remember. There are two men in my life whose cologne or after shave made me think early on "That's what a man smells like."

First, my dad. He wore several different colognes over the years, but always came back to one. I wear that scent exclusively today. Sam Melville is the other. I don't remember exactly what cologne he wore (I never asked), but I have a distinct memory of being close and having that sensory trigger. For all I know, he may have used the same cologne as my dad. It might explain why, deep in my memory, I've always had this father/son emotional bond with Sam.

I am left with the sense that he was a great father to his own children, if he had kids. Which, regrettably, I don't know. Or if I did, I don't remember. Wow, this all sounds so...sad. How can a man I barely knew still be a powerful memory, and yet, still such a mystery?

***

Stage 16 on the Warner Bros. lot is one of the largest stages in the world. The WB website touts its 2 million gallon water tank. The WB Tour will drive you past this massive building and give you the history of how it began as just another stage on the lot before being expanded for a film. All that is great, and I highly recommend learning more. But none of it compares to being inside when filmmakers are taking advantage of all that space. I was fortunate enough to get that chance while I worked on Scarecrow and Mrs. King.

No, we didn't film there. At least, I didn't film there. I'm pretty confident in writing that our little show about spies didn't have the need for the nearly thirty three thousand square feet of space available on Stage 16. They could have built all of Washington D.C. in there. No, I was on set as a guest during the filming of the feature Goonies. Specifically, the set of One Eyed Willy's ship.

Here's the thing about movie magic...It's just that, magic. Walking onto just about any set is like traveling through a dark tunnel to get to an oasis. The outside of the sound stages themselves are just plain, giant box buildings. One enters through a heavy steel door into what looks like the dusty old warehouse at the end of Raiders of the Lost Ark. Nothing looks new or clean or placed where it should be. In many cases, a person has to walk through catwalks and structures built up to form whatever set you're on. That was the case for Paul Stout and I on the set of Goonies. We walked through the door into catwalks. Up, into catwalks, through tunnels of steel and plywood.

The oasis of movie magic is where you emerge from those tunnels onto the set itself. Whether it's a half hour comedy or full-fledged movie set, walking onto a set the feeling for me is the same. Magic. The set of Goonies was all of that, and more. Imagine walking through a tunnel, climbing a flight of stairs or two, and then walking out onto a balcony overseeing a lagoon with a full sized, real life pirate ship! All inside of a building in Burbank, California.

It was pretty special.

We were on set thanks to Paul, who knew Mark Marshall, a production assistant on Goonies. Mark held various positions for Steven Spielberg's Amblin Entertainment, even serving as Spielberg's assistant at the time. The day we were there, the crew was busy staging Sloth's stunt of sliding down the mainsail with his pirate blade. To be able to see it in person, then on film, is something I'll never forget.

Of course, the other visitor to the set made the day that much more memorable. We'd heard a rumor, and as we were leaving had the chance to fully realize a dream. Paul and I raced through the catacomb of scaffolding and approached the two, rather large men in suits blocking our path. Our shouts of "Michael, Michael" were enough for the entourage to stop and allow us the brief moment to introduce ourselves and shake hands with Michael Jackson!!

His sister LaToya was there too, but we didn't get a chance to meet her. We did see the limousine out in front of the soundstage, though. Overall, not a bad day. How many kids my age could say they met the biggest star in the world on the set of a movie? Not many. I appreciate the things I've been able to do and experience.

I was able to spend time with more of the Goonies cast while they filmed in Burbank. I had lunch in the Burbank Studios commissary one day with Ke Huy Quan, the actor who played Data (as well as Short Round in Indiana Jones and the Temple of Doom). I remember him being exactly like his characters on screen. High Energy. We laughed a lot.

***

I did a made for TV movie called "And There Were Times, Dear", starring Shirley Jones and Len Cariou. The movie dealt with the impact of Alzheimer's on relationships, and was an important, albeit imperfect, discussion to be had. The medical field was still learning more about the disease, and the film ended up being a sign of the times as noted in several articles that later came out.

For me, it was an opportunity to play a young boy. Quite the stretch, I know. I remember being excited about filming something new, and even more so about filming somewhere new. If I recall correctly, all of my scenes were exterior shots, filmed on location. It's fun when you get to go new places, even if the subject matter is a serious one.

My mom's fondest memory of that production was one night we had a script read at Bob Hope's house, as his daughter Linda was one of the producers of the film. My mom, having grown up a fan of Bob Hope had been thrilled we had been in his house, and tried to impress upon me that fact during the car ride home. My reply?

"Oh mom, he's just a man."

That about sums up my understanding of the world around me. At twelve, I had no real idea of who Bob Hope was, and certainly wasn't impressed that I had just been invited to his house to read a script because I was about to be in a film his daughter was producing.

I think it's fair to say that I took the whole acting thing for granted when I was a kid.

***

Myron Natwick. I'm fairly confident I never worked with Myron on Scarecrow and Mrs. King, but again, fans will probably scream at me and tell me different.

Regardless, if I never remembered working with Martha Smith, I sure as hell don't remember ever working with Myron Natwick. In fact, my earliest recollection of Myron is from the 30th Anniversary Reunion in October of 2013. Just looking at him scared the hell out of me. He looks villainous, doesn't he?

Nothing could be further from the truth, though. Myron is the sweetest man, and over the course of a few years that we've gotten together for reunions and autograph shows, I find myself drawn to him. He has so many incredible stories, and is always warm and friendly and eager to share. I love that he is still working, and I look forward to seeing him any chance I get.

How Tall Are You?

When I walked into the room for the Scarecrow and Mrs. King 30th Anniversary Reunion and saw Richard Herd standing there, I was shocked. Honestly, I had no idea he was on the show. Forgive me, please. I just don't watch the show like the fans do. And I feel bad about saying that. I think until recently, I hadn't seen an episode in thirty years. I have them all on VHS, thanks to my mom, but I just never watched.

I knew Richard from Seinfeld. Which, for me, was great because that day I got to spend time with this wonderful actor whom I love as a peer, and he had no idea I was actually a fan. I mean, I told him I loved his work, but it was different. I love Bruce and Martha's work, too, but they're family to me.

By the way, Richard Herd is a cool cat. I loved getting to spend the day with him. Nothing makes me happier in this industry than spending time with down to earth people who are incredible working actors.

***

How Tall Are You?

Jean Stapleton was a guest star on Scarecrow and Mrs. King. I had known of Jean from her work on *All in the Family*, of which I was a fan. I first met her in Germany. How many people can say they met, had lunch and just hung out with Edith Bunker, in Germany? Not many, I feel safe in writing. But I did.

I remember she filled the room. Her personality was engaging, and her laughter and energy was contagious. I shared that lunch with Kate Jackson, Beverly Garland and Jean Stapleton. Three strong, smart, badass women. We laughed a lot. Do I have a picture of me and Jean, doing all that laughing? Of course not. I have a picture of my mom and Jean. I probably snapped the damn photo. Am I bitter? You be the judge.

***

The running theme, you'll see, is that I have no memory of a lot of these guest stars that fans love so much. Mostly because I didn't work with them, but also because I was a kid and my memory from my time on the show continues to disappoint me.

I worked an autograph show in Los Angeles in 2017 where the cast of Scarecrow and Mrs. King were featured guests. Bruce, Martha, myself, Myron and good friend and show producer Dennis Duckwall were all invited. So, too, was Stephen Macht, better known to the fans as The Wizard.

I know him as Henry Gerard from the USA hit Suits, starring his son Gabriel.

I'm not going to lie to you, I was about as excited at the opportunity to meet Stephen at the autograph show as I was being at the show itself. I'm a huge fan of Suits, I hate his character on the show, which means he is PHENOMENAL in that role because we're supposed to hate him, and well, I couldn't wait to meet him.

To be fair, I have stories of meeting celebrities where they failed to meet my expectations or worse, they're just assholes. I don't have enough to write a book about it, but it's pretty well known that some actors are full of themselves. I'm not a fan of those people, but I'm probably not going to tell you those stories. It's just not who I am.

I can't think of a celebrity, actor, athlete or otherwise, that I've met that *exceeded* my expectations more than Stephen Macht.

I mean, I didn't think he was the egotistical jerk he plays on Suits. I just didn't know he was this intelligent, soft spoken, funny man. If I had never watched Suits and was meeting him for the first time, I'd have never even known he was a career actor.

I want to leave you with this, and it may disappoint you. I have no interest in sharing my conversation with Stephen to you, if only because I want to selfishly hold onto it for myself. You know that feeling when you witness something like a sunset or a deer or something rare and magical and then afterward realize you had a camera in your hand and never took one picture? You're kind of disappointed, but mostly grateful that you didn't ruin the moment by trying to take a picture? That's my memory of having my first conversation with Stephen Macht.

I'd encourage you take an opportunity to see him at a convention or autograph show, and before you think to get a picture, have a conversation with him. Definitely buy something from him, but I guarantee the memory of your conversation will be more valuable to you than the autographs or memorabilia you'll most certainly walk away with.

***

How Tall Are You?

Jamie King began wearing glasses on the show because Greg Morton forgot to take them off of his face one time during filming. It wasn't written into the script that Jamie needed glasses. Greg Morton has bad eyes, and is not that cool. Also, I promise to stop writing about myself in the third person.

**

I distinctly remember a scene being filmed in the living room where the camera was set facing the kitchen. It was a bad day for me all around. I'd been wearing glasses since late 1984, maybe early 1985. I'd been wearing them because, well, I couldn't see anything. I was bumping into stuff, which makes it hard to get around. At night the streetlights would look like stars with big ole streaks coming off of them.

It could account for why I struggled in math class, but then again it could be because I just hate math.

Anyway, we were filming this scene, and I was supposed to go from one side of the room to the other, and instead of going the long way around, I cut in front of the camera, which, in case you didn't know, makes for horrible television when the viewers can't see through the 65 lb. monkey standing in front of the camera.

During the first take the director bellowed out a "CUUUUUTTTTTT!" and then I'm sure an exasperated sigh before telling me from across the room that I can't walk in front of the camera because I'm not invisible. I remember my face getting flushed and warm and feeling generally stupid.

I'm not blaming the director for making me feel that way, it was just how I felt. He was doing his job of directing a young man who had been doing this long enough to know better and yet, was having a bad day. On account of I couldn't see.

After that I put on my glasses. The rest is optical history.

Actually, I don't think that was the first time I wore glasses on the show. I think the first episode of Season 4, Stemwinder Pt. 1 is the first time I'm seen with glasses. A massive head, mudflaps for ears, unruly hair, mouth full of braces, no chin and glasses that look fresh off the face of a 72 year old newscaster.

How Tall Are You?

I just told you that other story because 1) it's true and 2) I told you I wasn't cool and you didn't believe me.

***

At one time I had Sal Mineo's wetsuit. Through the 50s, 60s and 70s, Sal Mineo was a famous actor, most notably as costar of the James Dean film *Rebel Without a Cause*. As I recall, Sam Melville gave me the wetsuit. But I wasn't sure. In researching this book, I've had numerous conversations with my mom for help. So, in not being sure about the wetsuit, I once again phoned a friend, so to speak. My mom couldn't really remember, but believed someone in the Wardrobe Department just gave me the wetsuit. Basically, she was of no help, and to this day I have no idea how I came to own Sal Mineo's wetsuit. Of which I no longer own. This story is apropos of nothing. At least, nothing interesting. Aren't you glad I'm writing a book about this stuff?

***

You've most likely heard of the game Six Degrees of Kevin Bacon, where in six moves any actor in Hollywood can be connected via film to actor Kevin Bacon. Yeah, you can play that game with me, too.

How Tall Are You?

A few years ago I started to connect myself to other actors, based on my time on Scarecrow and Mrs. King. Turns out, being in a television show with Kate, Bruce, Beverly, Martha, Mel and Paul put me just a few degrees from just about any actor out there. Go ahead, try for yourself. Play a few rounds.

To be fair, Martha worked with Kevin Bacon in Animal House.

That minor technicality aside, I will continue to remind folks that I worked with some true icons in the industry. I was the newb on Scarecrow and Mrs. King. I think you've found at least some of my stories prove that I didn't know what I was doing. Still, I did some amazing things, worked with some amazing people and lived to write a book about it.

***

I met Alyssa Milano at a Hollywood function one time. I don't remember how old I was, but Alyssa is only about a month older than I am so...

How Tall Are You?

Really, not a great Alyssa Milano story, I know. I just wanted you to know I met Alyssa Milano once. And that I thought she was cute.

***

I'd met quite a few actors my age that over the years have done some great work and have become well known. Brian Austin Green and I used to show up at a lot of the same auditions. Of course, now I think he's like, six feet tall. Not that I'm bitter.

I worked an autograph session with Danny Pintauro of Who's the Boss fame. He wasn't the cutest of the two kids on that show. That'd be Alyssa Milano. I met her once. You probably know this.

Jason Hervey and I also used to meet on a lot of auditions. He went on to later co-star in Wonder Years with Fred Savage. I've never met Fred.

I did meet Christina Applegate, though. I thought she was cute. She was, still is, but mind you I was a teenager and thought every girl was cute. Christina Applegate most likely did not feel the same way about me that I felt about her. In fact, like most people, she probably confused me for David Faustino, who played her brother Bud on Married...With Children.

I thought Winona Ryder was super cute. I never got to meet her, though. It's for the best, as I have no doubt she was probably taller than I was. I just wanted you to know I thought Winona Ryder was cute.

***

In 1984 I appeared in a commercial for Friendly's Ice Cream. Friendly's is a restaurant chain located mostly in the northeast United States (for those of us that have never heard of it). I don't remember the job, specifically, other than the prop master kept spraying hair spray on this perfectly good ice cream throughout the day to keep it "camera ready".

Hollywood can be such a cruel place.

UTOPIA NOW

For the record, I'm 5' 5" tall.

After finishing this book, I'll return to writing my Virgil "Bear" Ryan series of action/adventure novels. If you haven't already, I invite you to read the first two in the series, The Fury of the Bear and To Catch a Fox. I think you might enjoy them.

I have other books, too. They can all be purchased on Amazon or, if you'd like an autographed copy, can be purchased online directly from my website at www.MortonDesignWorks.com. I offer signed memorabilia, as well as other unique items I've designed, too.

I would imagine that most, if not all of you, have seen at least one episode of Scarecrow and Mrs. King. If you haven't, it's quite possible you still have no idea who I am and this entire book was very confusing for you.

It was a show about a divorced housewife and mother of two who got mixed up in the international world of espionage. The show aired from 1983 – 1987 on CBS. It starred Kate Jackson, Bruce Boxleitner, Beverly Garland, Martha Smith, Mel Stewart, Paul Stout, and me. All four seasons are available on DVD or online for streaming. I encourage you to check it out. If you've already seen the show or happen to be one of the many huge fans still active in the SMK community, well, then, this last paragraph was just a waste of your time.

From time to time I'm fortunate enough to still attend reunions for the show or other autograph shows. If you attend one that I'm appearing in, please take a minute to say hi, and let me know you've read this book (especially if you enjoyed reading it). If you didn't enjoy reading it, you can just say hi and leave out that other part.

For those of you still around who may be featured in this book as an author of one of my fan letters, please let me offer my sincerest gratitude and thanks. Your time and effort to reach out to me meant the world, even if some of you were just being greedy and wanted a picture. I'm kidding. You were all greedy and wanted a picture. I appreciate that, though. Honestly, I do. Because you wanted *my* picture. You could have asked for anyone's autograph (and many of you did), but you still wrote to me.

How Tall Are You?

If, for some unfortunate reason, you did not get an autographed photo in return for your efforts, please contact me via my website. I'll be sure to make things right.

For those of you that did get an autographed photo, and have held onto it, please please please reach out to me and let me know. I'd even love to see a picture. I'm sure more than a few of my return letters or autographs are cringeworthy and good for a few laughs. I'd love to see it and, if possible, share it with the SMK community.

For those of you who are fans I've met along the way or fans of the show who didn't write and haven't met – Thank You! Thanks for being a fan. Thanks for supporting my work on the show, and for many of you, supporting my work since. I love what I do, what I've done, and it is special that all of my work has found an audience somewhere in this great big world.

Wishing you all the best!

With love,

Greg Morton
(Jamie)

Acknowledgements

These things don't write themselves.

It takes the love and support of a lot of people to even consider writing a book. I'm fortunate enough to have these people in my corner:

My wife, Sandra. If I'm being truly honest, I do the things I do in life so my wife will think I'm cool. And hot. I'm not sure if it's really working or she just thinks my *attempts* are adorable. Regardless, we've been married for a long time and I'm a better man because of it. She's the love of my life.

My daughter Shelby. She always provides a unique perspective to our conversations, and has recently focused that insight on my writing. Pride. That's what I'm feeling when I realize my little girl has become a strong, intelligent adult. I've had to ask her to dumb it down for me when she offers critiques of my work.

My daughter Cameron always inspires me to dream big. Her love and support help encourage me to take risks and keep chasing those dreams. I hope I make her proud.

My mom and dad. Even though mom is in a different time zone, and our lives are busy, we make time to chat on the phone. Our conversations haven't changed much in the nearly forty years I've been trying to make her laugh. Still, she worries and I brush her off like any snot-nosed son. It's our thing. I continue to hear her life lessons long after we've hung up the phone. My dad, too. He's been gone a few years now, but still influences my life every day. I got lucky with those two.

My brother Jeff is a good man. Sometimes I'm amazed how mature, smart and driven he's become. And then we talk on the phone and he acts like a 13 year old and it takes me back to being a kid. It's the same, but different. Better.

I want to say thanks to Kerstin Kern for her help in reviewing this book. Kerstin has been a friend for a long time and whom I love dearly. I know she's a friend because she isn't afraid to be honest with me and tell me when I'm wrong. It doesn't happen often.

David Johnson knew I was writing this book, but didn't know I was writing *this* book. Thanks for the conversations, the laughter and the support.

I want to thank Taya Johnston for her support and friendship. Taya currently hosts the Mrs. King Chronicles Podcast online alongside Lexie Fiema, Jenn Peterson and Miranda Thomas. Thirty years after SMK went off the air and this squad is still talking about it. Thanks for inviting me to your zoo.

I've known Eric Tunforss for over twenty years. Every time we chat (which isn't often enough) he asks me if I'm writing. I think about that nearly every time I sit down in front of my computer. Eric, I appreciate your friendship. By the way, I think Eric is like, 6'1". I don't have short friends.

I *am* the short friend.

Other Works

Poetry

The Untitled Poems

Fiction

The Fury of the Bear

To Catch a Fox

A House in a Field of Reeds

Non-Fiction

Lifting a Foot Forward: A Lesson in Balance

Visit

www.MortonDesignWorks.com

to learn more

Printed in Great Britain
by Amazon